SUMMER

Anomie   FRESTONIAN GALLERY

Introduction

From the publication of the first edition of *The Anomie Review of Contemporary British Painting* in 2018 through to the third in December 2024, Anomie has set the benchmark in identifying and critically reviewing those British-born or based painters whose work has significantly impacted both the domestic and international scene. The anthologies have provided a thoughtful, cohesive and beautiful series of captured moments in time that, together, describe a truly remarkable breadth and depth of artistic talent at work (and play!) in Britain today.

Matt Price of Anomie has been the driving force of that project, penning volumes one and two himself before being joined by a fabulous host of writers and curators in assembling the monumental volume three: Amah-Rose Abrams, Melissa Baksh, Holly Black, Lauren Dei, Yasmina Floyer, Anneka French, Matthew James Holman, Kathryn Lloyd and Anna McNay. Shaping the assembled texts and images, the understated and elegant design by Joe Gilmore completes the picture of what is already a record of some note in living art history.

At Frestonian Gallery, we have long been fans and friends of Anomie, and a curatorial collaboration has been a much desired and discussed aspiration – and yet *SUMMER*, this resulting exhibition, has exceeded even our highest hopes. The two dozen artists featured in the show represent a prime cross-section of the vibrant and ever-developing contemporary painting scene that has been the core focus of Frestonian's programme (and correspondingly our own heartfelt passion) since the doors at our Holland Park space first opened in 2017. Two *SUMMER* artists – Jessie Makinson and David Price – appeared in our inaugural exhibition, and several others have since joined the Frestonian stable. All involved are painters whose extraordinary work we have followed and enjoyed for many years.

Far from creating an atmosphere of increased competition and protectionism, the rise and rise in recent years of social media and the expansion of the artistic environment to a truly integrated global scene have provided a stage for artists to cross-promote, critically inform and celebrate one another's practices – nowhere more evidently than in contemporary British painting. We are grateful for the support, collaboration and enthusiasm for the exhibition from all the featured artists and their gallery representatives. It is in this spirit of celebration and promotion of excellence across a broad spectrum of generations, backgrounds and styles that Frestonian Gallery and Anomie Publishing feel very privileged to present *SUMMER*, and we hope you will enjoy the exhibition.

Rollo Campbell & Matt Incledon
Directors, Frestonian Gallery, London, June 2025

SUMMER
Matt Price

1. Quintessentially British (and Other Fictions)

The British summer is not known for the sweltering, unbreathable heat of the Mediterranean or the Middle East, where many British people choose to go for their holidays. It is, perhaps, better known for warm, gentle evenings spent pottering around the garden, trying to keep the lawn green and the flowers alive – the kind of garden you might find in Tim Braden's painting *With reds and pinks and purples and mauves* (2025). Braden uses the paint sparingly over the soft, creamy-pink ground that primes the canvas, and the mark-making is also spare, as if made with just a couple of different brushes. This economy of means, as with all great painters, only serves to make the overall effect more magical: how can these reserved yet uninhibited brushmarks, each almost entirely separate from the others like little islands of oil paint, create such a coherent and charming evocation of an English country garden? The lilac flowers dominating the foreground are handled in a similar way to the leafy green tree some dozen or so metres away, bringing a unity and flatness to the picture plane – the loaded brush allowed to run dry with the relaxed confidence of someone in full control of both their subject and technique. Some dark rectangles are all that's needed to tell us that a beautiful house lies beyond the idyllic garden. The title gives the clue that's needed to figure out the location – a line from Virginia Woolf's notebooks describing the gardens at

Charleston House, once home to Bloomsbury Set painters Vanessa Bell (1879–1961) and Duncan Grant (1885–1978). The garden was designed by artist and critic Roger Fry (1866–1934), one of the circle of friends and visitors who made the well-trodden journey from Bloomsbury in London to East Sussex. 'Through the windows shown across the flowering gardens is Virginia Woolf's writing room,' explains Braden. 'The painting derives from a black and white photograph of the now famous gardens there.'[1]

Taking us from the south-east of England to the south-west, Hannah Brown's *Day for Dusk (Coast Path) 1* (2025) depicts an early summer's evening stroll along a country lane – the South West Coast Path – in Cornwall, looking down on Polzeath Beach. It is a path well known to Brown, who has visited this popular tourist destination every summer for over twelve years. It is, however, Brown's first ever painting of the sea. 'The view across the Atlantic felt timely in light of current geopolitical events, with the effects of decisions made thousands of miles away rippling out across the world,' she says. Followers of Brown's oeuvre will know that she regularly depicts hedgerows – the narrow strips of woodland separating fields and lanes that are so essential to the wildlife and biodiversity of the English countryside, first created by Bronze Age farmers. Since the Second World War, up to fifty percent of hedgerows have been lost in parts of the UK, and it wasn't until the 1990s that this began

1   All notes provided by the artists for the *SUMMER* exhibition and catalogue, 2025, unless otherwise indicated.

to be reversed.[2] Brown's painting gives us an up-close and intimate view of dense foliage contrasted with the infinity inferred in the horizon between sea and sky glimpsed beyond, somewhere between daytime and evening: 'I started the *Day for Dusk* series in 2021; the title references "Day for Night" cinematography – scenes set at night are filmed during the day using a blue filter to simulate night-time. Instead of a blue tint, I use a brown/purple glaze to suggest dusk.'

Caroline Walker presents an image of a different – though familiar to many – type of summer holiday in her painting *Scoops* (2025). '*Scoops* is part of the series *The Holiday Park*, which takes as its subject a British family-friendly holiday park where my family and I spent time last summer,' explains Walker. 'This particular scene shows a young woman in the "Scoops" ice-cream shop.' In making this painting, Walker brings together two key themes of her practice in recent years: family life – particularly motherhood – and women at work. As anyone with young children who has been to a holiday park will know, the facilities are designed to offer a safe and convenient environment for leisure, sport and entertainment, and alleviate some of the day-to-day pressures on the parents. In the painting a young woman is tasked with serving ice-cream – perhaps a summer job, perhaps it's all year round. We don't know much about her – whether she's a local or has travelled far for work, what her mother tongue might be, what her own family situation is, whether she is happy. But here she is, doing what she's paid to do, helping to make the customer's holiday as enjoyable an experience as possible. Let's hope that the ice-cream's good. Walker's seemingly breezy painting style captures the matter-of-factness of the moment with all these questions circling in the sweet and sugary air. The details of the server's life are, quietly but unmistakably, inseparable from wider social, economic, gender and political questions in Walker's remarkable oeuvre.

Few things, perhaps, could be more synonymous with summertime in Britain than tennis, epitomised by the strawberries-and-cream sunny days and rainy days of Wimbledon. British tennis somehow carries with it an almost religious sense of tradition and decorum, strictly implemented rules and protocols, like a hangover from the days of the British Empire, not to mention the public school-like uniforms and PE kit. In *Some Sort of Commotion* (2025) Jessie Makinson doesn't stand upon ceremony when it comes to tennis, however, turning a game that appears to have started with the best of intentions into a curious farce. One woman has either accidentally fallen on top of, or deliberately knocked over, another, pinning her down with a (tennis?) elbow to the neck. Lying in the middle of a grass court replete with immaculate straight white chalk lines, the rivals are surrounded by fluffy tennis balls as if one of those tennis ball machines has gone rogue. There are pleated skirts, bare legs and stripy white socks akimbo, the posture of the woman on top a conscious nod to the oddly posed woman playing the titular card game in Balthus's *La Patience* (1948). It's the Balthus reference that gives this otherwise playfully ludicrous scene its slightly uncomfortable, mildly erotic, not-quite-rightness. In Makinson's super stylised world,

2   RSPB, 'Hedge History', rspb.org.uk https://shorturl.at/ILqUR (accessed May 2025).

this strange, almost animalistic interaction (a cat with its prey?) is a compositional and aesthetic tour de force, and surely one of the most memorable tennis-themed paintings by a British artist of all time.[3]

2. Looking At, Looking Away

A single figure is depicted in an elegant and understated untitled work by Gideon Rubin – a woman viewed from behind. Her hands are placed on her shoulders, just starting to take off, slowly and gracefully, the whitish-grey dress she is wearing. There is bright light on her from above, leaving pronounced shadows on her flesh and clothing. Perhaps it is a warm, sultry summer's evening and she can't wait to get out of her day clothes. Rubin has also previously referenced the work of Balthus, so there is sometimes a keen, if not furtive, sense of someone being watched in his paintings. Here, it is we the viewer who are made to feel like the person watching, a voyeur perhaps, entering someone else's personal, private space, and it's unclear whether we have been invited. Rubin's refined, subdued palette takes its cue from the understated brown linen support, loosely painted over with a khaki wash. From this flat, muted background comes forth the sculptural volume of the dress, enhanced by the chiaroscuro and the bold, gestural brushstrokes. The woman's auburn hair and pinky-yellow flesh, while harmonious with the rest of the palette, lift the painting from the monochrome into colour – the beauty of the tilted head, neck, shoulders and arms bringing humanity to the body and life to the painting.

Jonathan Wateridge also presents a painting of a woman viewed from behind. She is walking into the night, brightly illuminated in the foreground, as if in the light from an open door, the headlights of a car or the powerful flash of a paparazzo's camera. She is, perhaps, walking on light stone chippings on the drive of a country house or restaurant, though curiously her feet are absent, giving the impression of floating. Her head raised a little, she stares into the distance, where tall tree trunks and foliage are silhouetted against a night sky. Two bright though blurry patches of yellow and white are like lamps or camp-fires in the middle distance, though it's hard to know for sure, lending an element of ambiguity, a sense of the unknown, to the scene. The woman is wearing a minty-green evening or party dress, casting strong black shadows on the tops of her calves and shoulder blades. Her bare arms indicate it's a mild evening, and we are left wondering where she is going – is she on her way to a party, or trying to escape from one? Bright flecks in the sky, among the trees, suggest a hint of excitement, drama or even tension in the air. Titled *Long Weekend* (2025), the implication is that this is a mini-break, a summertime adventure – the kind of evening away we might dream of, or that stays in our memories – yet there is perhaps an underlying sense of danger or menace here. Indeed, Godard's film *Week-end* (1967) – a film Wateridge himself admires – is more of a nightmare than a dream. While Rubin's painting focused on the three-dimensionality of the woman's body, Wateridge's does the opposite, reducing his subject's physicality to flattened planes and abbreviations verging on modernist abstractions.

3   For a tennis-themed contemporary art Instagram feed, see tennis.art. collection

The exhibition's third *rückenfigur*, or figure depicted from behind, is by Lindsey Bull, in a work titled *Purple Cape* (2025). A woman (probably though not unequivocally) sits on a bench looking out onto what appears to be a coastal scene, though it is so faintly rendered in delicate washes of yellows, oranges and reds that it is impossible to be certain. What is clear is the fiery red hair, glowing yellow on one side, that falls down her neck onto a striking bright purple cape. Where the shadow is darkest, at the base of her spine, it becomes a deep, vivid purple, giving a vibrant cobalt-blue reflection on the bench. The intensity of pigment here is the exact opposite of the bleak, empty sky. It's a wistful, possibly melancholic or maybe just tranquil scene, though we can't help but wonder who, or what kind of person, this might be. A cape is often an intrinsically theatrical item of clothing – as if the person wearing it is somehow in character, like an actor or a model. Perhaps this is the kind of clothing this particular person wears all the time. 'In all my works I am trying to explore the beauty and drama of a moment in time,' says Bull. 'There is an introspection to the figure as well as assertion. I find it interesting to couple a sense of fragility with a deep sense of confidence in the figures.'

3. From Elsewhere to Eternity

Kaye Donachie presents the work *Folded Sunset* (2025), which depicts a woman's face, neck and shoulders in an ethereal floral dress in delicate pastel colours. While the title evokes the lines from the poem 'Questions of Travel' (1965) by Elizabeth Bishop (1911–79) – 'And have we room / for one more folded sunset, still quite warm?' – Donachie made the painting after reading the director's notes by Marguerite Duras (1914–96) for her play *Savannah Bay* (1983). The play features just two parts – a retired actress and a young woman – and revolves around the older woman's fading, changing recollections of a love affair and death involving a third woman that connects the two characters. The figure in Donachie's painting could be any of the three women at different moments in time, conveying a gentle demeanour of melancholic reverie, reflection and regret. Donachie explains the painting in her own words: '[Duras's] descriptions are edited and simple, but her ability as a filmmaker and author presents strong intertextual images, merging elements of her life and memory across fiction and reality. In this painting, these nuanced interwoven narratives form the basis of my own reimagining of a character or actor. I wanted the figure to exist in a space where they simultaneously emerge into the light and fade into darkness. The colours are warm and tonally close, the light is intentionally ambiguous, being seen as both the sun and stage light to heighten an emotive sense of time and place.'

Leading us from Donachie's painterly romanticism to true romance, a couple are caught embracing in the corner of Minami Kobayashi's *The copper hair and cherry blossom trees along the river* (2025), in front of a river-bank, with branches of pink blossom hanging over a brick wall and out over the shimmering water below. While arguably more associated with spring than summer, the blossom and blue sky make us think of warm, endless days and the 'eternal summer' of blossoming love. But all is not quite as it seems, as Kobayashi explains: 'The painting was inspired by an intimate scene from the movie *Blade Runner 2049* (2017). In it, a hologram woman with artificial intelligence synchronises with a real woman's body and kisses a man; the two women's bodies nearly overlap, but never completely, thus it is a sad scene. [...] There is a river in my hometown, and there are miles of fully bloomed cherry blossoms in spring. I miss the beauty of these flowers and their short, fragile lives.'

Also bridging the seasons for love is David Price's *Vertumnus and Pomona after Anthony van Dyck* (2025). Originating in Ovid's *Metamorphoses*, the story goes that one summer, Vertumnus, the god of seasons and change, disguises himself as an old woman in a cunning plan to woo Pomona, the goddess of fruit and gardens, in her orchard. Among the thicket of intense, colourful marks, the figures can be made out in roughly the same positions in which they appear in Anthony van Dyck's (1599–1641) painting of the story from c. 1624, including Cupid sneaking off stage right, taking his bow and arrow with him.

While on the subject of deities, Daniel Crews-Chubb presents *Study of a Figure II (Immortals)* (2024) – a mixed-media work from his extraordinary *Immortals* series which invites consideration of the ideas of gods and immortality throughout history and across civilisations. Among many sources of inspiration, the sculpture of pre-Columbian cultures from South America often appears in his practice, leading us to think here of Xochipilli, the Mesoamerican god of summer, not to mention of pleasure, love, feasting, dancing and creativity. Crews-Chubb's image is a glorious cacophony of abstract marks and colours out of which comes forth a standing but weary-looking humanoid figure – perhaps at the end of a long summer's night of revelry. Xochipilli has famously been depicted surrounded by psychotropic plants and hallucinogenic mushrooms, so it's quite possible he's a deity familiar with altered states – a different kind of summer trip...

4. Paradises Lost and Found

Further mythical royalty is to be found in Ryan Mosley's *Sunflower King* (2025), a verdant walled garden in which a bearded man peers into a lily pond. In the foreground, jutting out into the centre of the canvas, is a monkey on the branch of a tree, staring at the man. In the bottom left-hand corner, a cat stands on the rim of the pond, contemplating an imminent attack on the golden carp swimming beneath the lilies. Apart from the minor drama going on in the animal kingdom, it is an otherwise peaceful scene, the towering pink wall pretty much blocking out the rest of the world beyond. In the bottom right-hand corner are the sunflowers over which this king reigns, a conscious nod by Mosley to Van Gogh, the lilies naturally evocative of Monet. The influence of Impressionism on Mosley's curious and colourful universe is clear in the swirling and uninhibited mark-making. In part inspired by the artist's imagination, the painting is also informed by a local farmer's pumpkin patch which, Mosley explains, 'adapts and changes its harvest seasonally to growing sunflowers when the weather allows'. It is a work, Mosley says, that has been 'painted with a fondness for the feeling of sunshine, sunflowers and that reassuring summer haze'.

The exotic imaginary is also at play in *The Artist's View* (2025) by Freya Douglas-Morris, in which a far-away land of purple, white, moss and mustard-yellow mountains surrounds a perfectly still cherry-red lake. The branches, foliage and blossom of a tree – possibly a silver birch – dominate the upper half of the canvas, like a pattern from a vintage silk kimono. Between the branches, a large peachy sun fills the sky with sherbet-yellow light. It is a landscape unlike any we might find on Earth, yet there is evidence of human life here, as Douglas-Morris explains: 'I have used the same tin to hold my brushes for many years. It's an old tomato paste tin from our local pizzeria. Incorporating this element into the landscape created an additional layer of narrative. The tubes of paint, brushes, cloth – it is as if an artist had sat sketching the view and has just left the scene. This concept reminded me of other artists who have used such a device, the painter painting the painting – Peter Doig, Caspar David Friedrich, Vermeer to name but a few; except in this version the artist has just stepped out of view, leaving only their painting materials visible on the hillside.'

Another seemingly imaginary landscape has been depicted by Nick Goss in *Paradiso Island Approach* (2025), only this time it is very much rooted in reality, as the artist shares with us: 'The starting point for the painting is a series of sketches I made when on a trip to Italy last year. We went to Lake Iseo in northern Italy, in Monte Isola. In the middle of the lake was an abandoned hotel left to be reclaimed by the elements. Hotel Paradiso looked like it was a grand place once, but now ivy and creepers were starting to move across the façade and into the windows; the whole place felt dwarfed by the forest behind.' In Goss's painting, it feels like an overcast day, the wind blowing through the tall, dramatic trees behind the hotel. In the foreground a figure rows a companion in a boat towards the abandoned hotel, as if in a scene from a film or novel. Summer holidays are not always the dream holidays we hope they will be, and Goss's hotel speaks of dream holidays that once were.

An unusual and immersive landscape appears in Kathryn Maple's fantastical watercolour, *Inside Out* (2025). As Maple elucidates: 'Over the past year I have spent a lot of time thinking about the landscape. Having made a show in 2022 in which the human figure was prominent, I have been thinking about what the space and surface of a drawing or painting can hold when the figure is removed, and what makes up a landscape.' The painting is a dense, dark but richly colourful depiction of a jungle-like forest or ancient woodland. It might look somewhat unorthodox or unrealistic until you google the specific trees she's depicting in this work: 'Something I have been looking at are the root systems of the Swamp Cypress tree. As much above ground as below, these strange lumps populate the land much like members of an orchestra, allowing each voice to come through at different times. [...] Keeping the drawing on the surface and exploring new ways of mark-making, I attempted to weave these obscure forms (called "knees") and their environment as a starting point […].' These trees, native to the south-east of the USA but which can grow happily in the UK, are as weird and wonderful as Maple's rendering of them, a visual symphony played by the orchestra of strange trees, perhaps.

5. Home and Away

Cara Nahaul's *Reverie #12* (2025) mixes up ideas of the far-away and home, depicting a luscious tropical landscape inspired by the island of Mauritius, from where the artist's father and his side of the family originate. A red-hot sun hangs in the lemon-yellow sky, and it is unclear if the horizon below meets a light, pastel-pink sea, a beach, a blank wall or a large building, as regularly pop up elsewhere in this body of work. Nahaul is interested in the island's colonial history and indentured labour there, not least as they are significant to her own family's heritage. A tropical paradise is rarely left untouched by matters of power and money, untroubled by outside forces, and Nahaul's idyllic, peaceful, timeless scene invites us to consider Britain's colonial past and its legacies.

Matthew Krishanu's painting *Boy Swimming (Wave)* (2025) also partly references a personal family history. Krishanu, of dual British/Indian heritage, spent a proportion of his childhood in Bangladesh. In his painting practice, Krishanu often reflects on his childhood experiences and the trips his family would take during the holidays. In this painting, a boy can be seen swimming in a deep-blue sea in front of an imposing, if not treacherous, dark ground – perhaps rock or a night sky. The boy is swimming by himself into a sizeable wave, so while there are joyful notes here they are more than matched by underlying dangers and melancholia. 'I have memories of swimming at night – when the tide is rough. I love the pull of the sea,' Krishanu comments. His pared-back imagery and broad, thin glazes of oil and acrylic paint enhance the sense of introspection and tension.

6. Rooms with Views

Anna Freeman Bentley's painting for the *SUMMER* exhibition revolves around a house in the Middle East that was once owned by a man who would travel the world for work, bringing back all kinds of souvenirs from wherever he went. After he died, his house became a museum, which was then hired as the location for the feature film *My Driver and I* (2024), about a Saudi girl's rapport with her chauffeur, produced by Caspian Films. Freeman Bentley, whose practice focuses on interiors, architecture and ideas of artifice and truth, was given access to the set and to other rooms in the house for a week during the filming process, resulting in a major body of work titled *Complete Reality*.[4] Describing the painting, Freeman Bentley states: '*Garden tableau* [2025] presents a mix of real and false vegetation staged around a window. In front of the plants is a theatrical proscenium arch, establishing a sense of distance from the ornaments on display. This idea of tableau is further conjured by the staging of images

4   A publication of the *Complete Reality* body of work was published by Anomie in 2024.

of birds of prey on the walls, alongside the branched horns of shooting trophies that sit in juxtaposition with the lush greenery. A diorama sits on the edge of the stage with what is perhaps a cuckoo clock, repeating this notion of staging and pattern. The light of the chandelier works with the light from the window as hanging ornaments and flowing pearls glisten throughout the arrangement of a space that bridges indoors and outdoors.' It is a captivating painting bustling with characterful visual information to stimulate the eyes and mind.

Also featuring a prominent window is Barry McGlashan's *No Particular Night or Morning* (2025). The title references a short story of this name by Ray Bradbury from 1951 that follows the psychological drama between characters on a long interstellar journey. The source image, however, is an old photocopy of the first known still-life photographic image – a heliograph by the French inventor Nicéphore Niépce, from 1822 – of a table setting. 'My version has been copied over and over,' says McGlashan, 'so has slowly degraded with each grainy reproduction – for me that has added a quality which a cleaner version would be missing. I used it as the starting point for this painting, a view from an open window.' Painted in whites and blues, it has the feeling of the aforementioned Day for Night photography or film – sunlight being made to appear like moonlight. While it is hard to decipher exactly what lies outside the open window – land or water, clouds or icebergs (or sculptural water features?) – it is clearly a tranquil scene, perhaps capturing the so-called blue hour, before sunrise or after sunset. McGlashan's charming and

otherworldly imagery, which references *fin-de-siècle* painters such as Bonnard and Vuillard, is a delightfully eerie evocation of just another midsummer's night on planet Earth.

Sunyoung Hwang's *Flash On* (2025) is an abstract work that evokes (for this writer's mind's eye at least) a window with dark red mullions and grilles and numerous glass panes seen through billowing, diaphanous multicoloured curtains. Outside, a sinuous, bright-green summer landscape is matched by a baby-blue sky and a deep magenta sun, low on the horizon in the valley between two hills. Hwang doesn't make preliminary studies for her paintings, preferring a more organic, impulsive process when working directly onto the canvas. Writing for her 2024 exhibition at Frestonian, Hwang described how 'My initial marks on the canvas are a starting point for a development of ideas and images for amorphous landscapes and a journey through them. Using a spontaneous, stream-of-consciousness method of composition, I overlap multitudinous layers with intuitive conceptions of time and space. This results in gestural works that feel like they have been caught in a moment – the ideas and emotions expressed can never be finished nor fully come into being, only (barely) contained by the canvas.'

Windows also play a role in Jai Chuhan's *Mirror III* (2024), bright sunlight and outside greenery – perhaps even a flower-filled garden – intimated by the abstract reflections in tall wardrobe mirrors of this intimate interior scene. Chuhan's thick impasto marks both define and obscure, leaving us with little certainty about the details of what we are looking at, yet with vivid impressions of it. The room is quite possibly a living room, though more probably a bedroom, a bed (or sofa?) with bright red bedding in disarray, like the aftermath of a hot and uncomfortable night. A female figure lies naked on the edge, her right knee bent with her left hand holding the heel of the foot. The woman's long dark hair falls onto the bedding. It's unclear if she is asleep in this awkward posture, or writhing around, tormented or in some other heightened emotional state. It's possible that the mirror referred to in the work's title is actually describing the position we hold as viewers, and that this is some form of self-portrait. This would mean that what appeared to be wardrobe mirrors might actually just be windows, rather than reflections of windows, and the gaze one of self-reflection as much as external observation.

7. Summertime Sadness

The painting by Des Lawrence depicts two yellow flowers in bloom surrounded by green leaves. I am no botanist, but my suspicion is that Lawrence might have picked Sequestered Sunshine – a form of peony that enjoys sunny positions – specifically for this summer-themed show. Followers of Lawrence's practice will know, however, that one of his major ongoing bodies of work is the *Obituary Paintings* series, of which this work is one. The title, *Obituary Painting: David Hessayon* (2025) gives the name we need to identify the person being remembered – a gardener, writer and long-standing chairman of Pan Britannica Industries, a garden and agricultural chemicals firm. Better known to many as Dr DG Hessayon, he is generally considered the best-selling author of gardening books to date, exceeding fifty million copies sold worldwide. Born in 1928 in Salford, Greater Manchester, he died in hospital, near his Georgian home and twenty acres of landscaped gardens, in January this year, at the age of ninety-six. Anyone who has a bottle of Baby Bio in their home will have a little piece of Hessayon helping their plants to live and thrive. Lawrence's realist painting techniques teeter on the brink of hyperrealism yet always retain something painterly and hand-made about them. It is the human touch that corresponds to the humanity his *Obituary Paintings* find in the lives of those he chooses to represent.

In a similar way to Lawrence's painting, Gareth Cadwallader's weird and wonderful watercolour *Long Gaudí* (2024) is also a form of memorial. Back in 2006, Cadwallader made a drawing of a relief sculpture called *Death of the Righteous*, located in Antoni Gaudí's Sagrada Família Cathedral in Barcelona. The sculpture shows a woman holding a baby at the bedside of a dying man. Years later, in 2022, the artist experienced the loss of his father just weeks before the birth of his first child. This series of events lent the old drawing a renewed significance, and it became the starting point for a new painting – one that was started but never finished. Then in 2024, while working on a series of watercolours based around similar themes, Cadwallader revisited the subject again, this time adding a curious architectural structure, with the repeated motif of a mother and child appearing in several decorative roundels.

In the foreground lies a strange organic form, somewhere between a mollusc, a pupa and a medieval wood carving; its ecclesiastical, cocoon-like appearance perhaps evoking themes of loss and rebirth. This painting, in some ways deeply personal, presents an esoteric life-cycle, a memento mori of sorts – all rendered in Cadwallader's distinctive, highly meticulous and detailed style.

Sadness and melancholy are emotions regularly depicted in, or evoked by, the paintings of Justin Mortimer, who has spent much of his career creating apocalyptic images of a dystopian world. In *An Uncertain Afternoon* (2025) Mortimer had started out with the intention of making a painting of an informal afternoon with family members, friends or neighbours 'enjoying a hot afternoon' in a regular domestic garden. But Mortimer's imagination is always, ineluctably, drawn to danger and tragedy: 'In the top of the picture the sky was darkening, ominously, and I was thinking of an unseen fire up in the hills behind this suburban scene.' At one stage, there were various figures in the painting, but Mortimer became dissatisfied and overpainted them with heavily applied paint, scraping off some sections and inadvertently removing some dry sections in the process. 'It was a mess. Out came the rags and I wiped the whole thing down. The solvents took with them all those details and all the figures. I put the panel away.' But all was not lost. 'A few days later I took it out and could see that all these bad-tempered erasures had brought something unexpected and helpful. The unnecessary had gone and what was left was a fragmented, brittle image far more interesting than what I could have achieved by careful working. The smoke in the sky was gone, yes, but the picture retained a peculiar atmosphere – fogged, as if regarded through an obscured lens or diseased eyes.' The balletic figure in the foreground, posed as if watering the garden or placing a towel down to sunbathe in front of the cataclysm playing out around her, was the last thing he painted. 'The previous occupants were tanned and warm, ochre almost. She, I decided, had to be grey-green and, importantly, unaware of the trouble unfolding behind her.' The title is an oblique reference to the short story 'The Sudden Afternoon' (1963) by JG Ballard (1930–2009), which revolves around a man losing his grip on reality. Mortimer's painting is the most depressing yet extraordinary and accomplished painting of a summer party imaginable, bringing our *SUMMER* exhibition to a spectacular end of days – a party to end all parties, you might say. Now where did we put the Pimm's…?

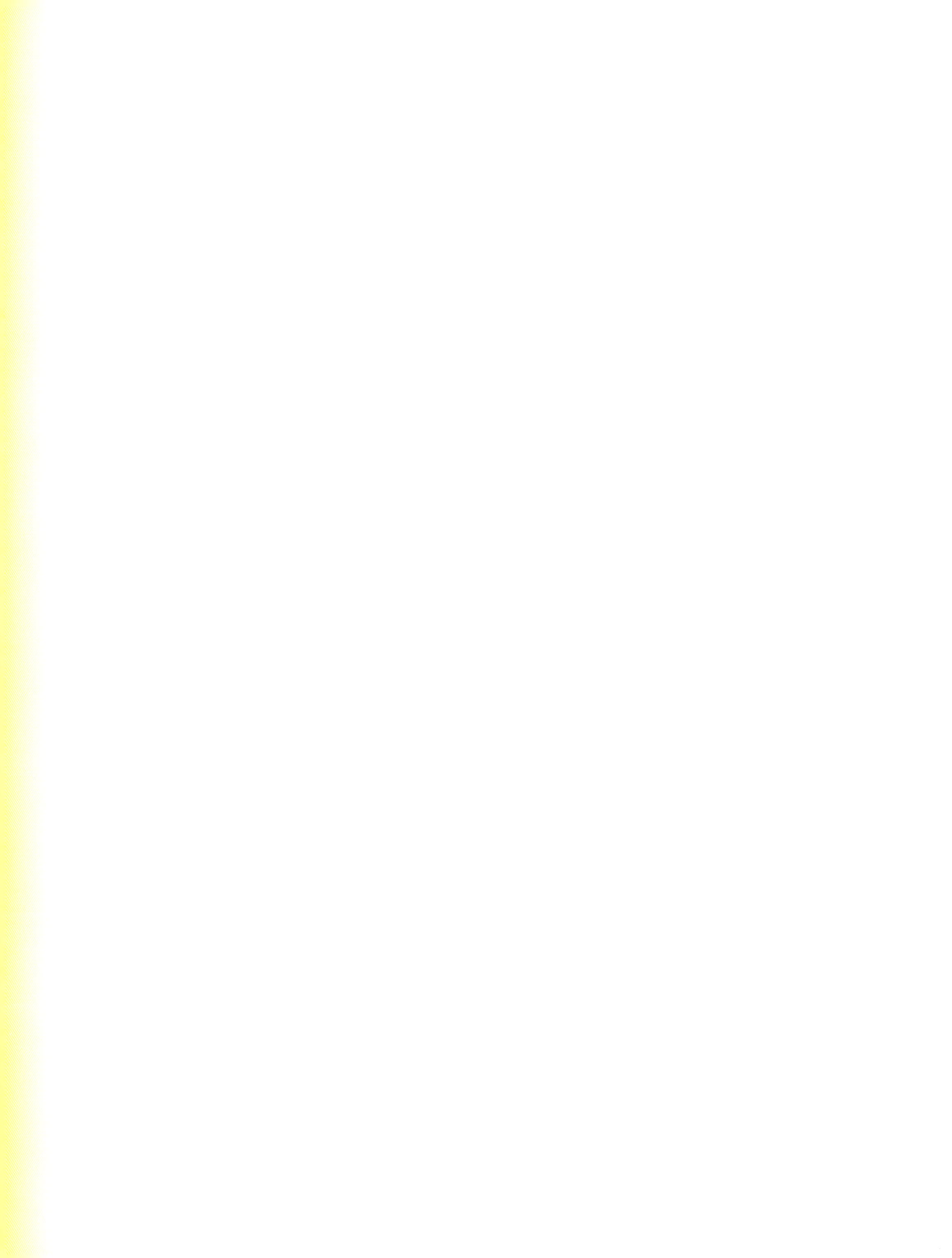

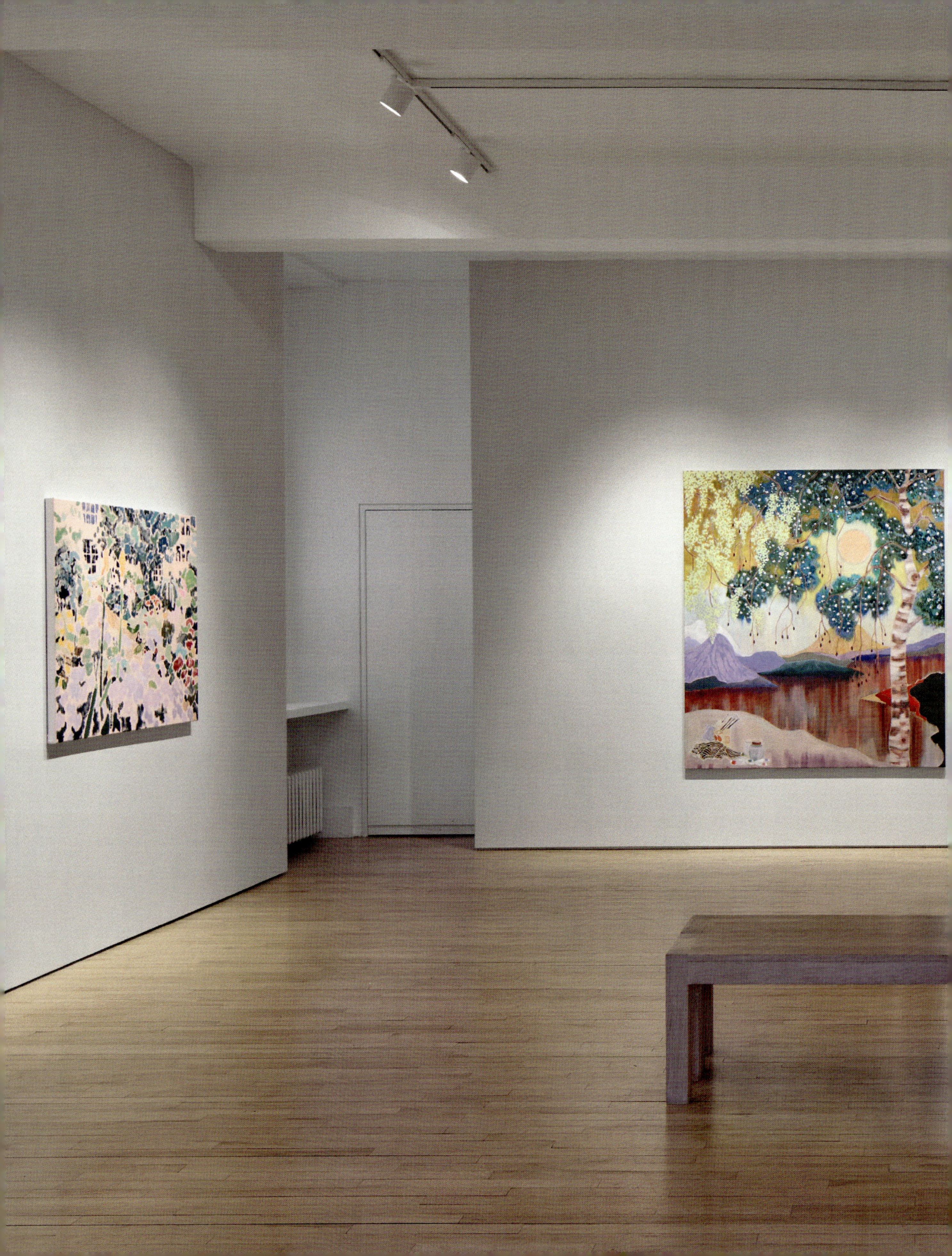

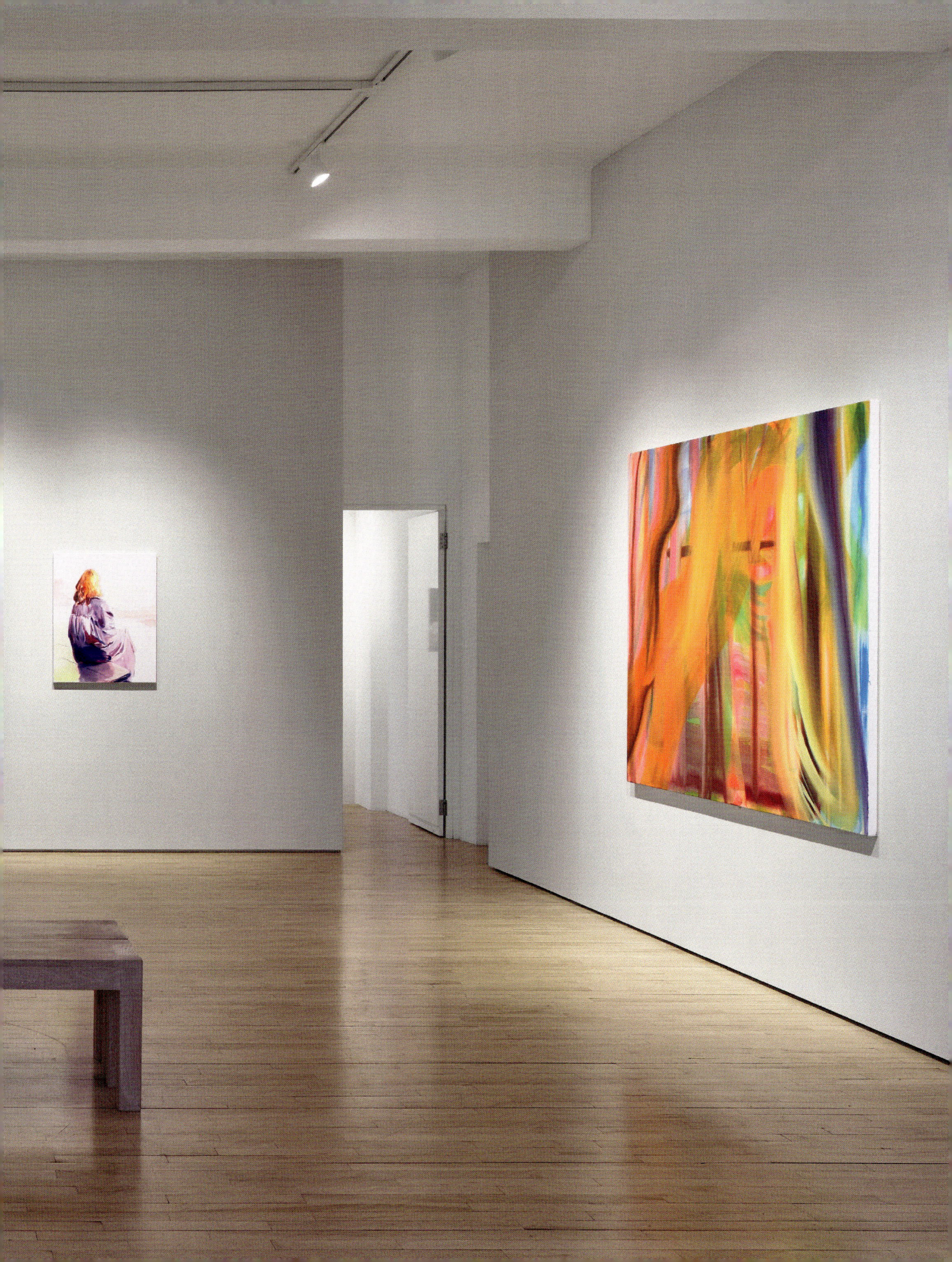

Tim Braden

*With reds and pinks and purples
and mauves, 2025*
Oil on canvas
100 × 130 cm
39⅜ × 51⅛ in.

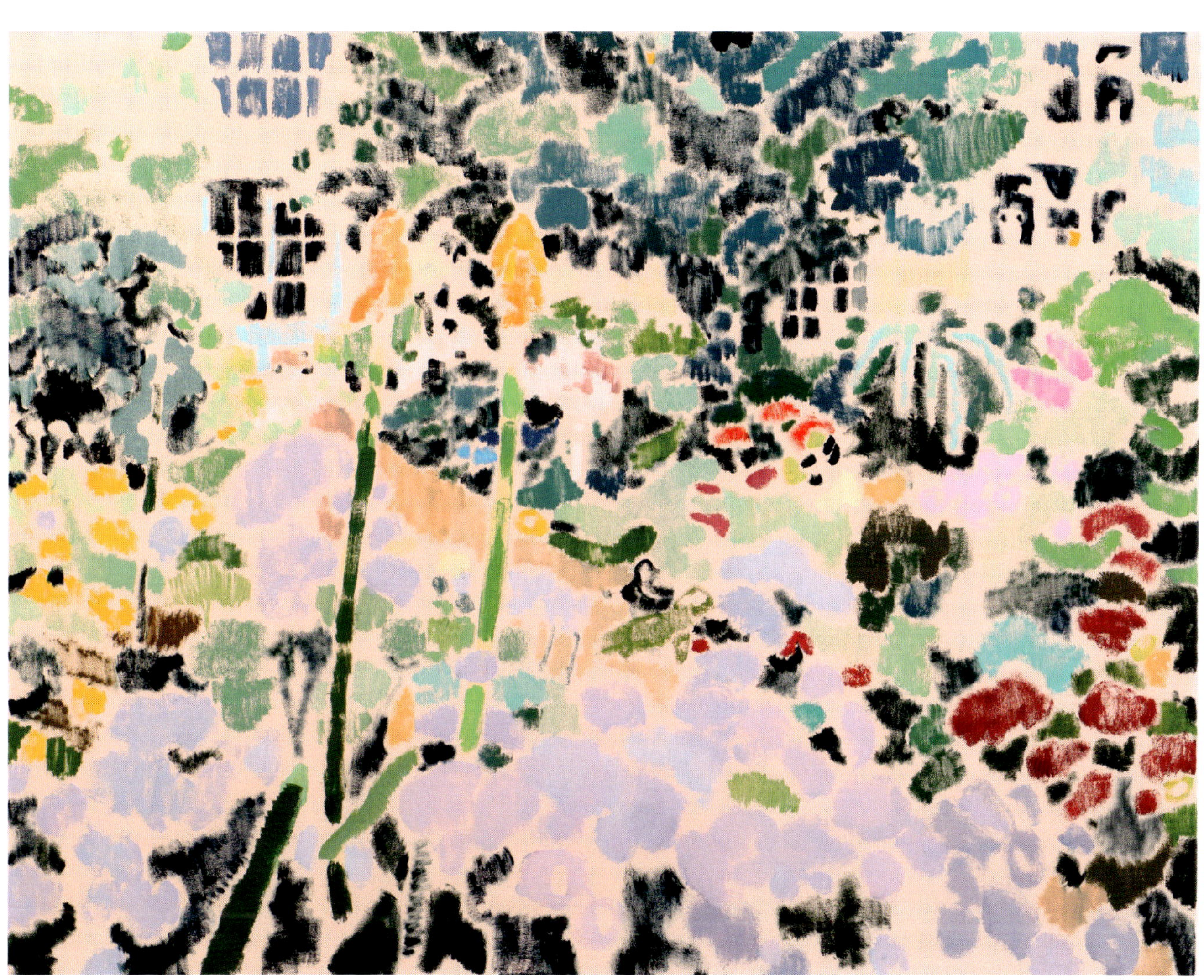

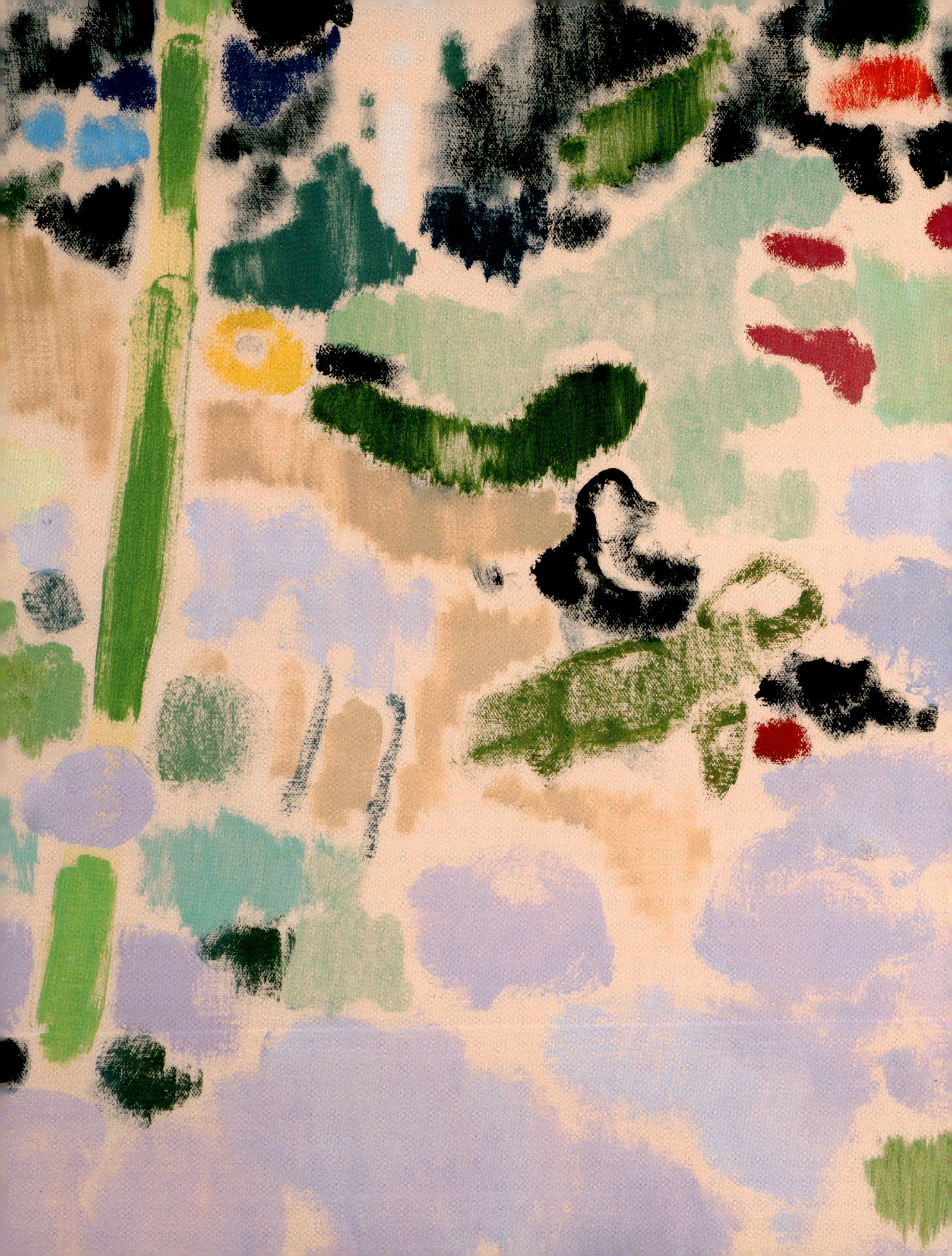

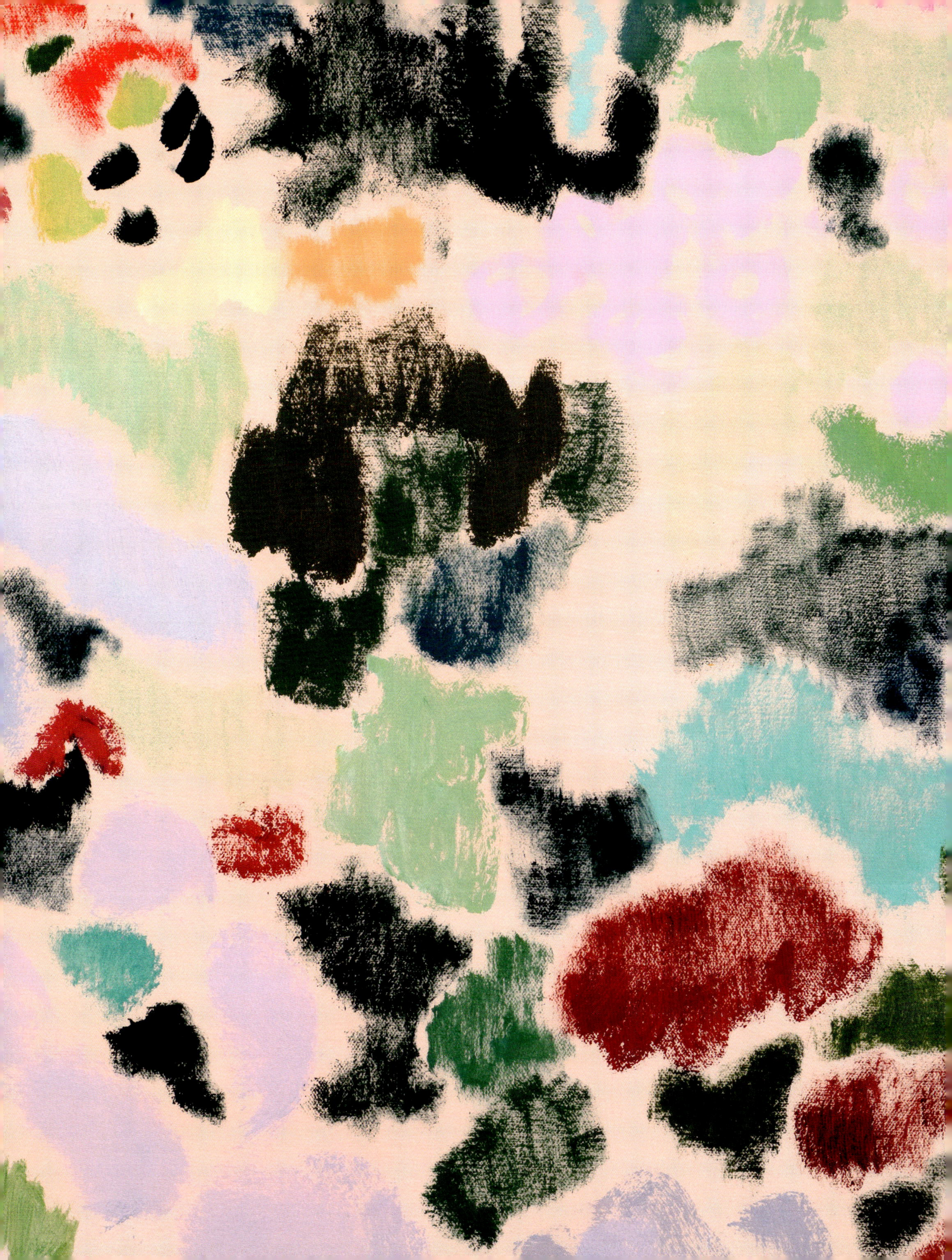

Hannah Brown

Day for Dusk (Coast Path) 1, 2025
Oil on canvas
100 × 90 cm
39⅜ × 35⅜ in.

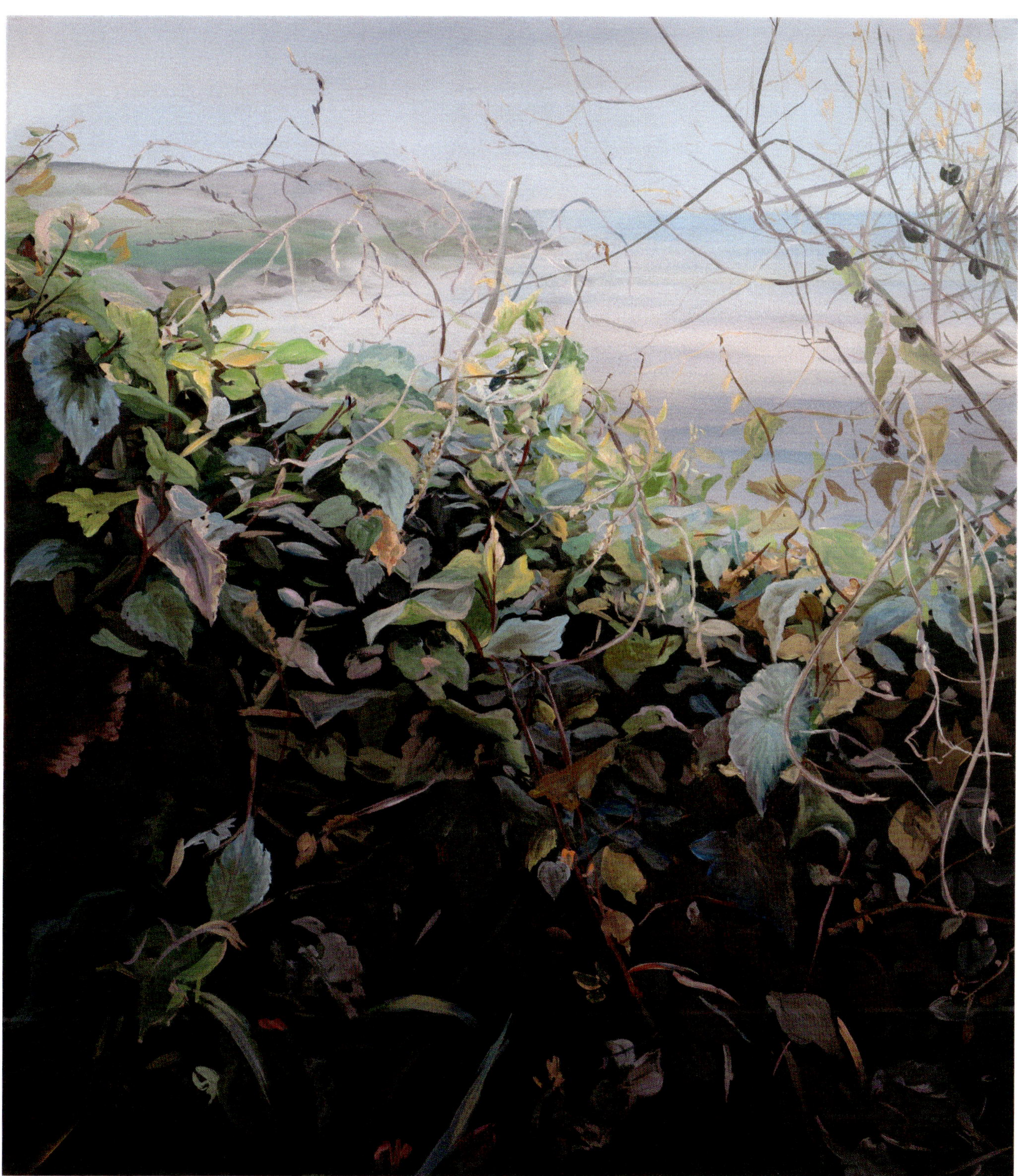

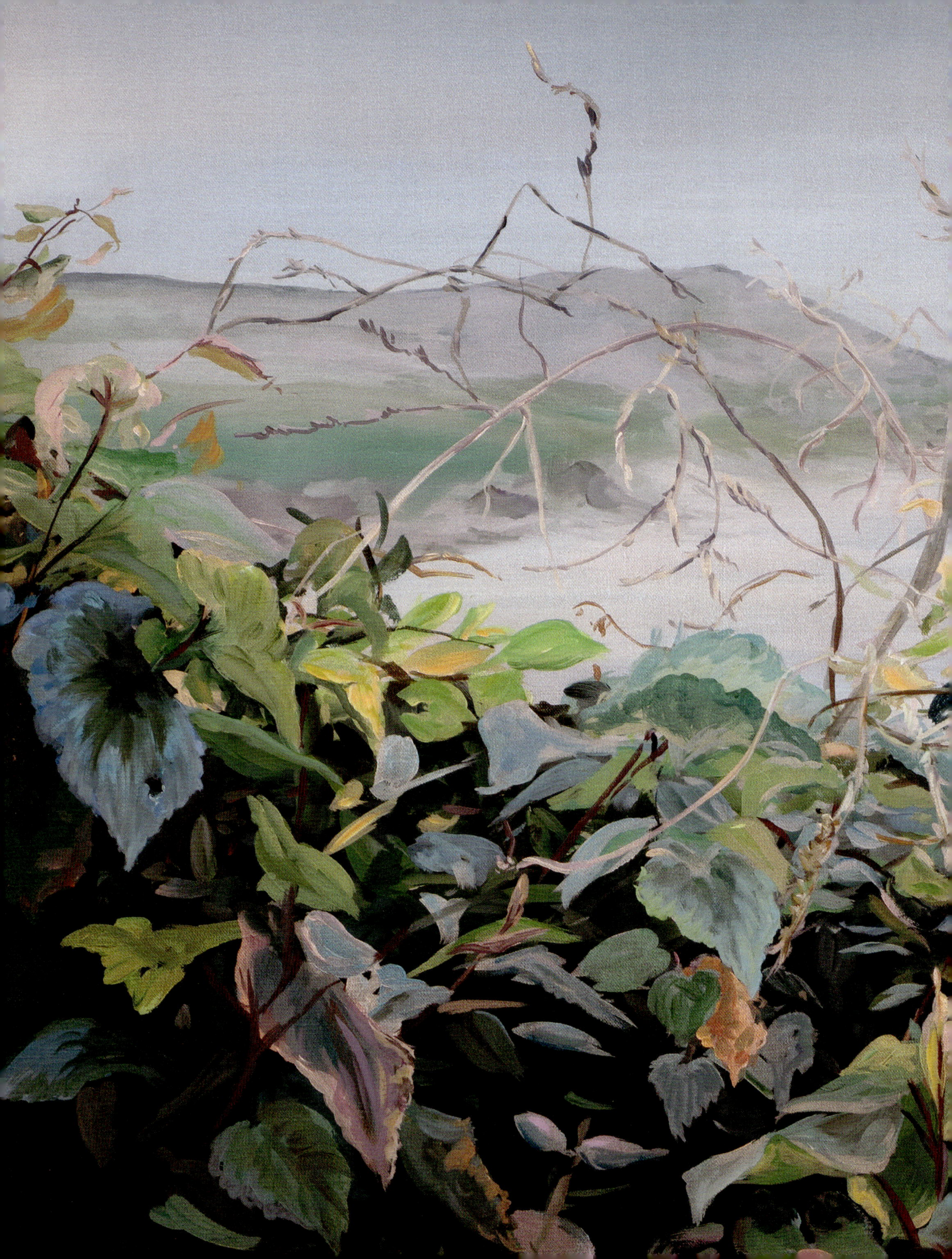

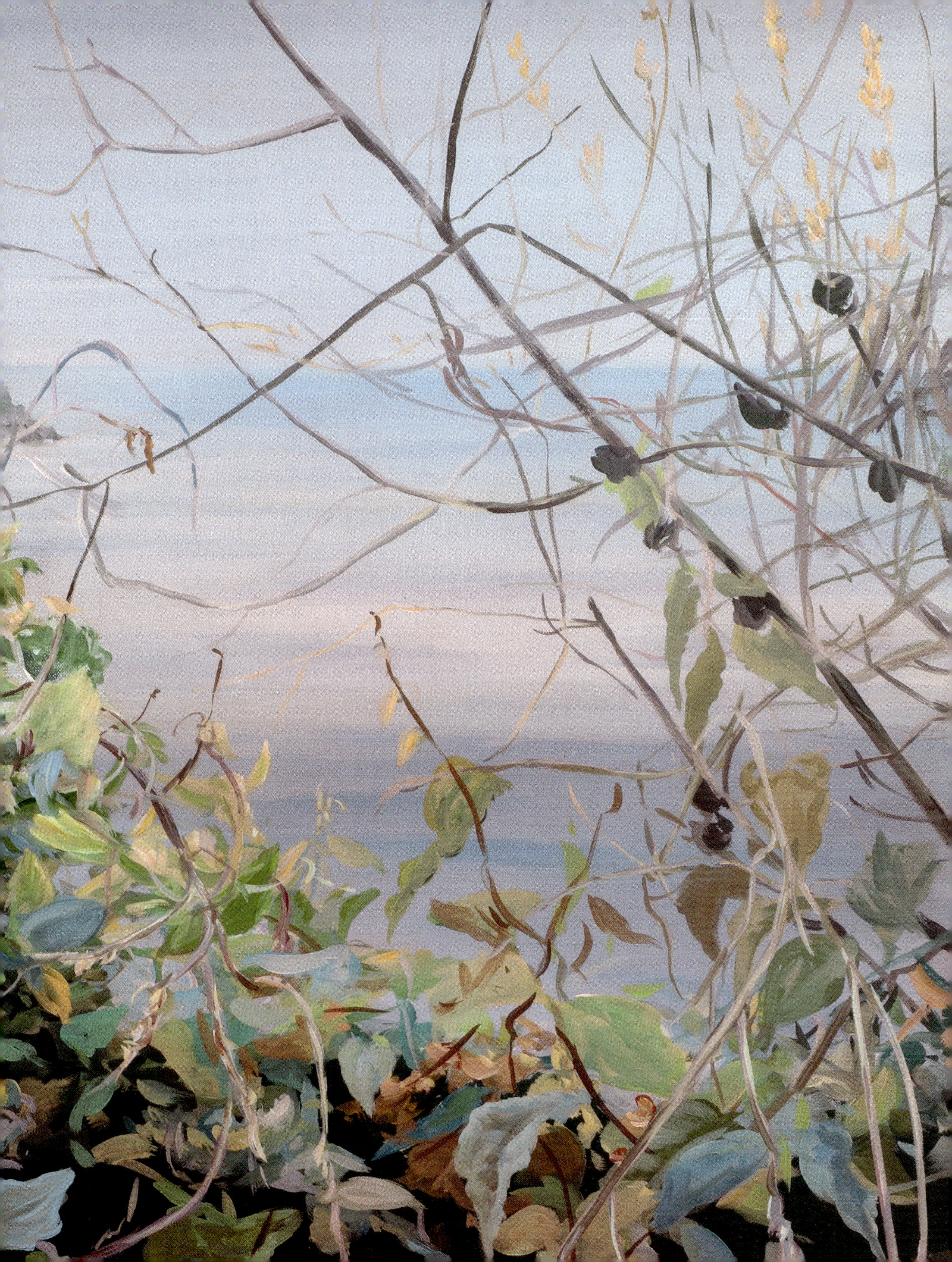

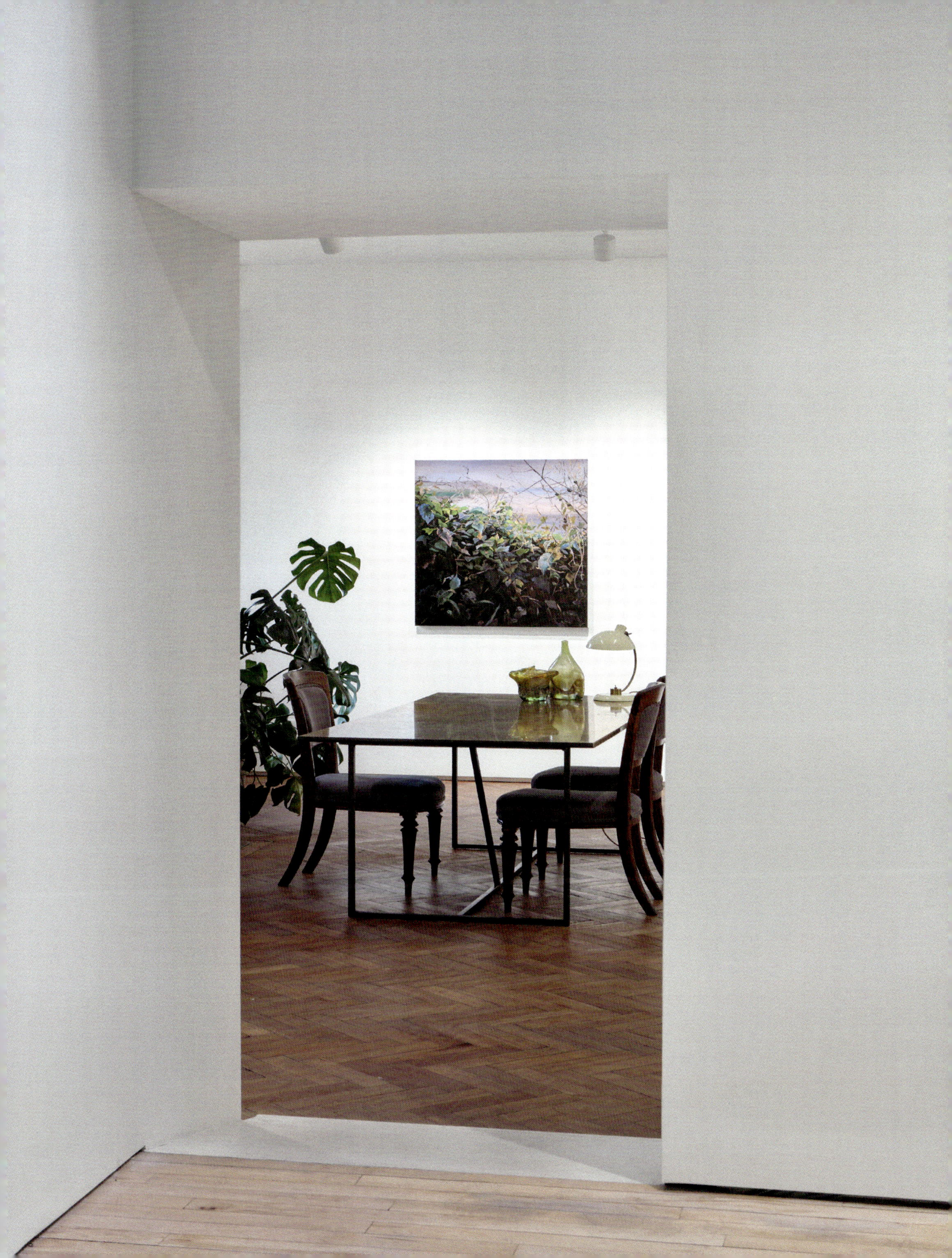

Lindsey Bull

Purple Cape, 2025
Oil on linen
80 × 65 cm
31½ × 25⅝ in.

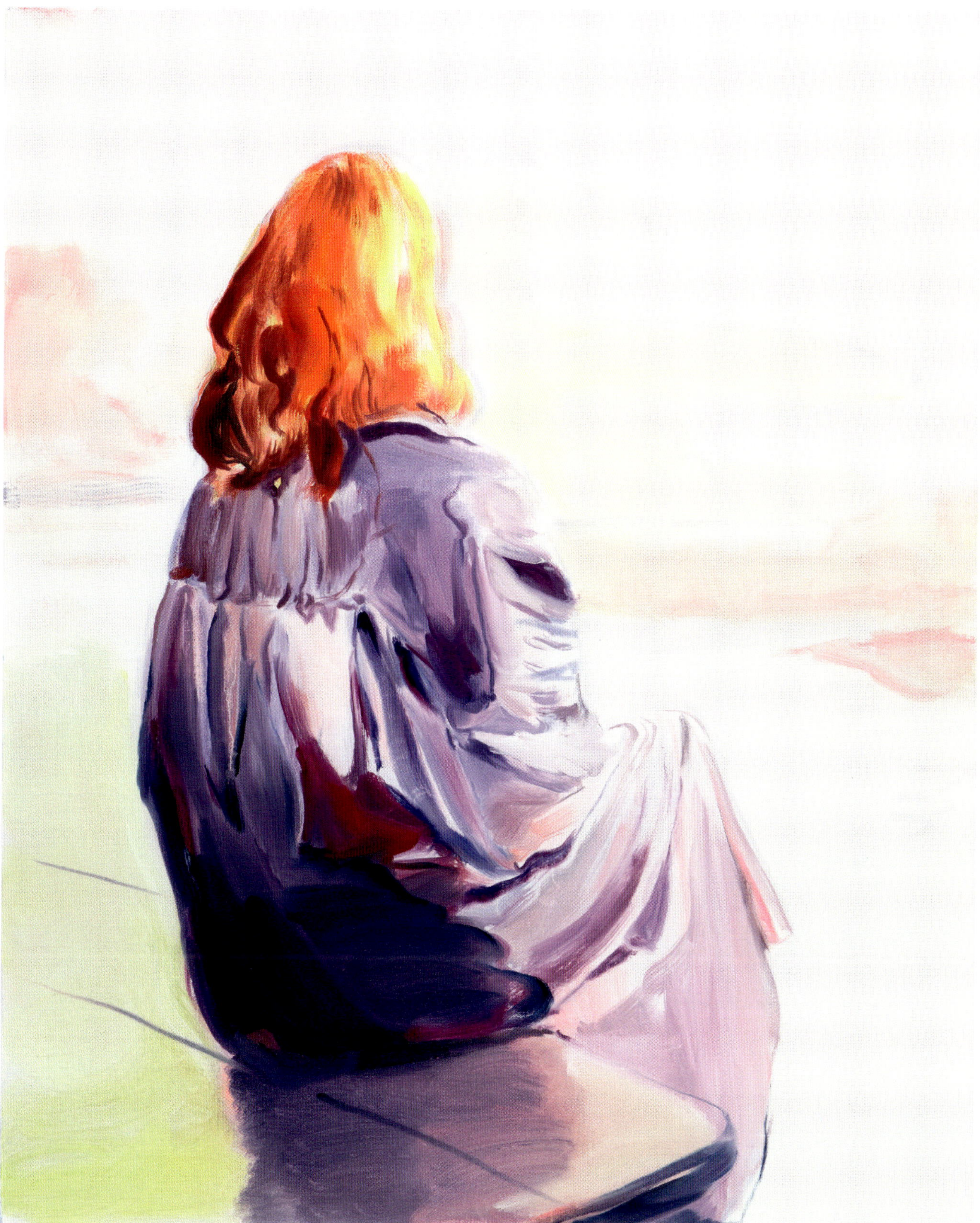

Gareth Cadwallader

Long Gaudí, 2024
Watercolour on paper
15.8 × 39 cm
6¼ × 15⅜ in.

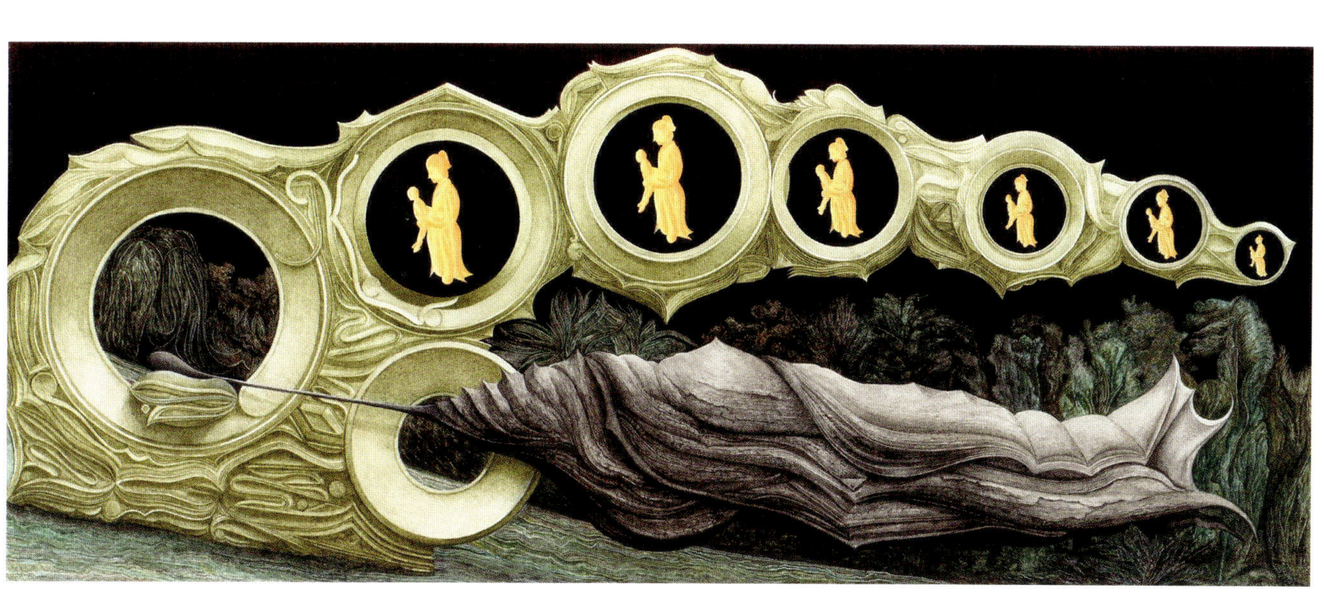

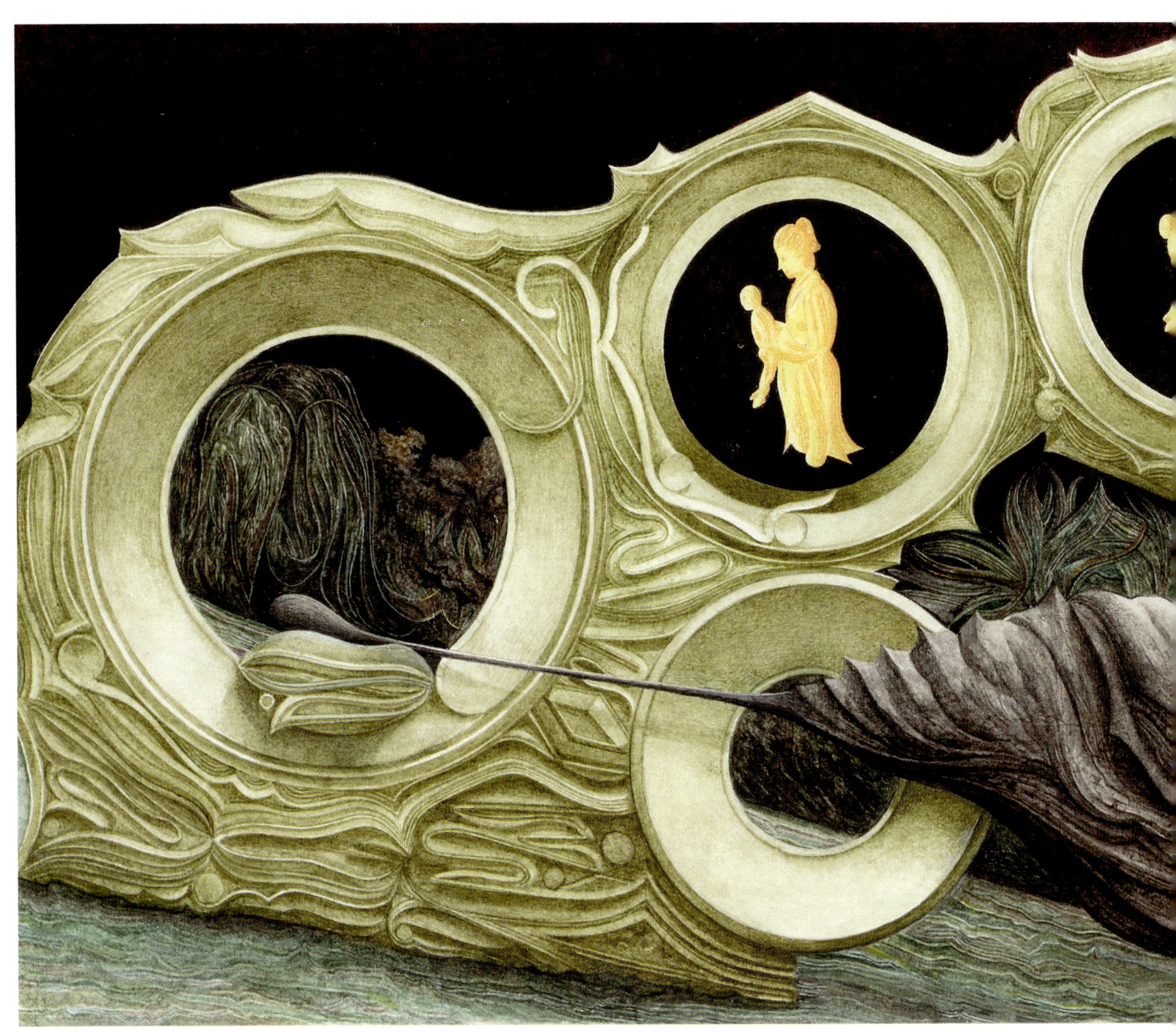

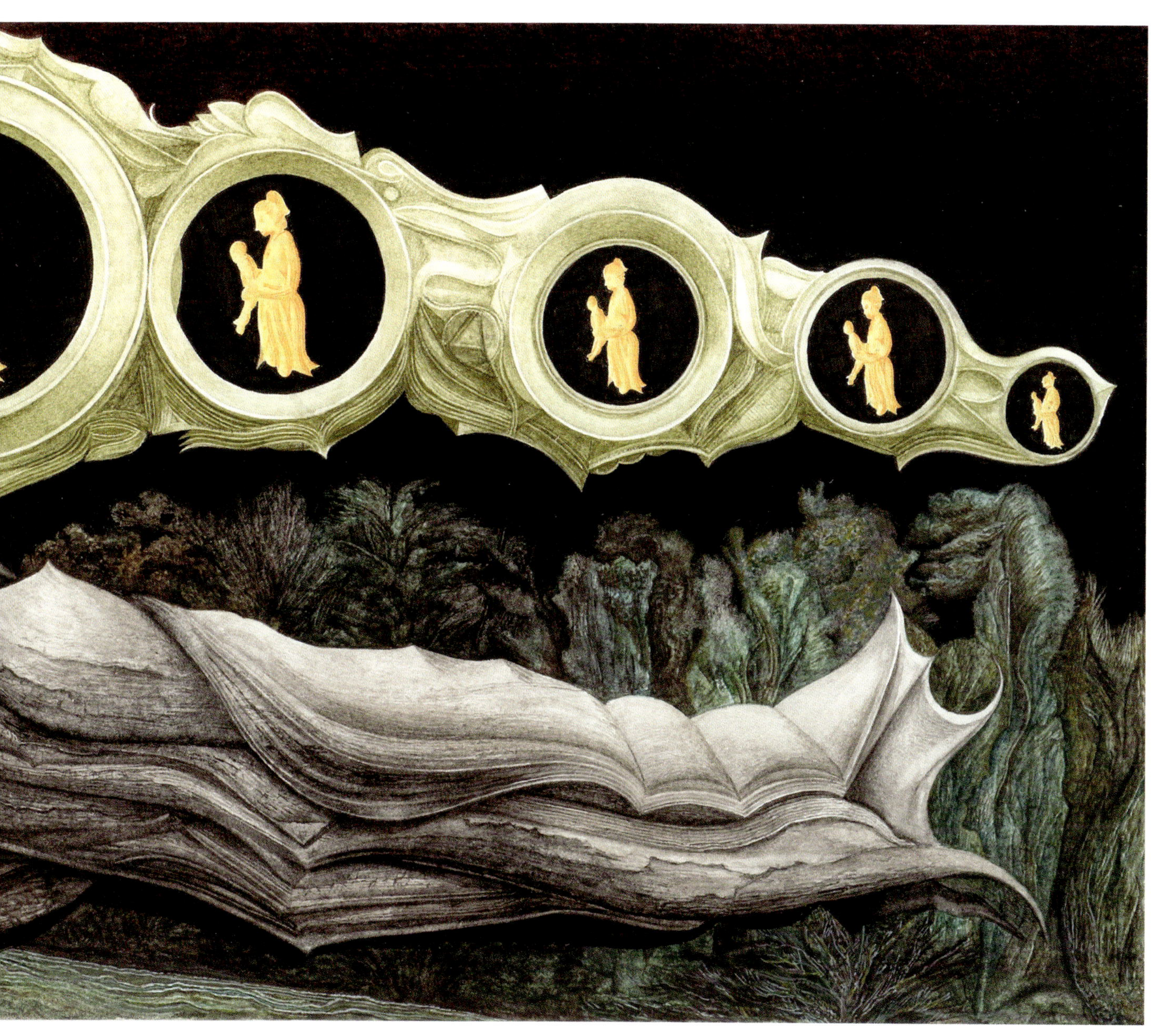

Jai Chuhan

Mirror III, 2024
Oil on canvas
51 × 40 cm
20⅛ × 15¾ in.

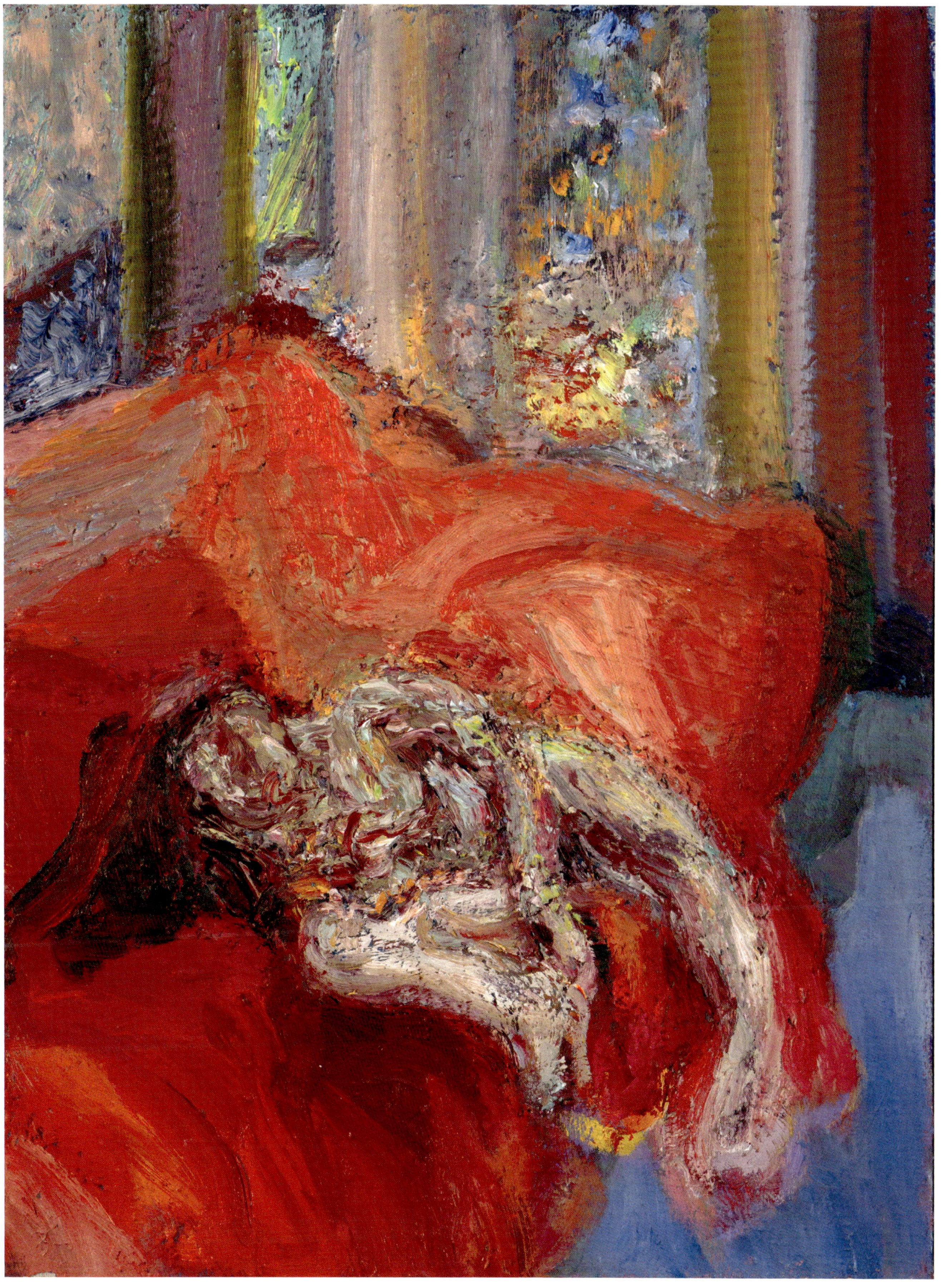

Daniel Crews-Chubb

Study of a Figure II (Immortals), 2024
Charcoal, acrylic, pigment stick, ink,
sand and spray-paint on paper
75.6 × 56.5 cm
29¾ × 22¼ in.

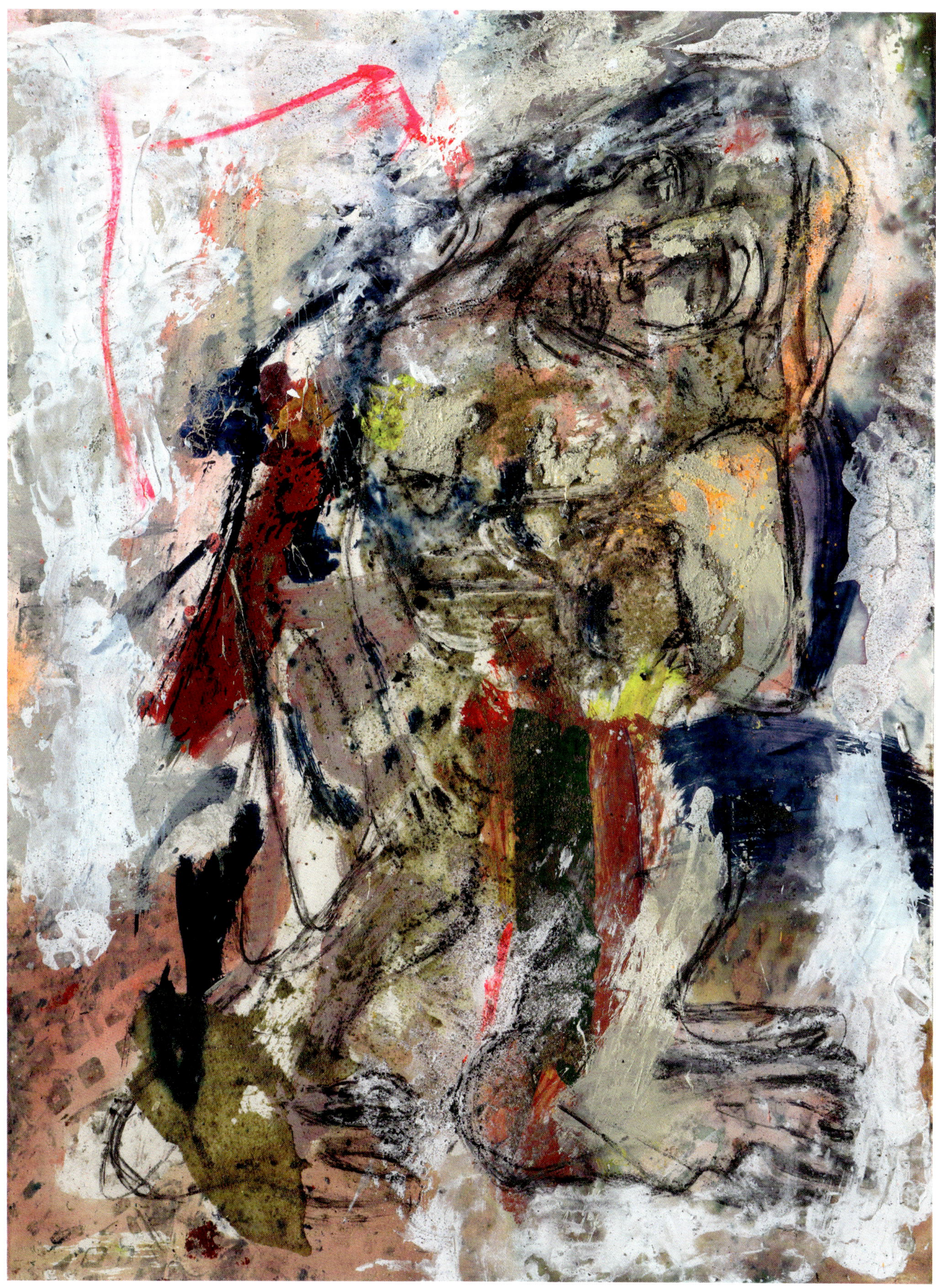

Kaye Donachie

Folded Sunset, 2025
Oil on linen
46 × 36 cm
18⅛ × 14⅛ in.

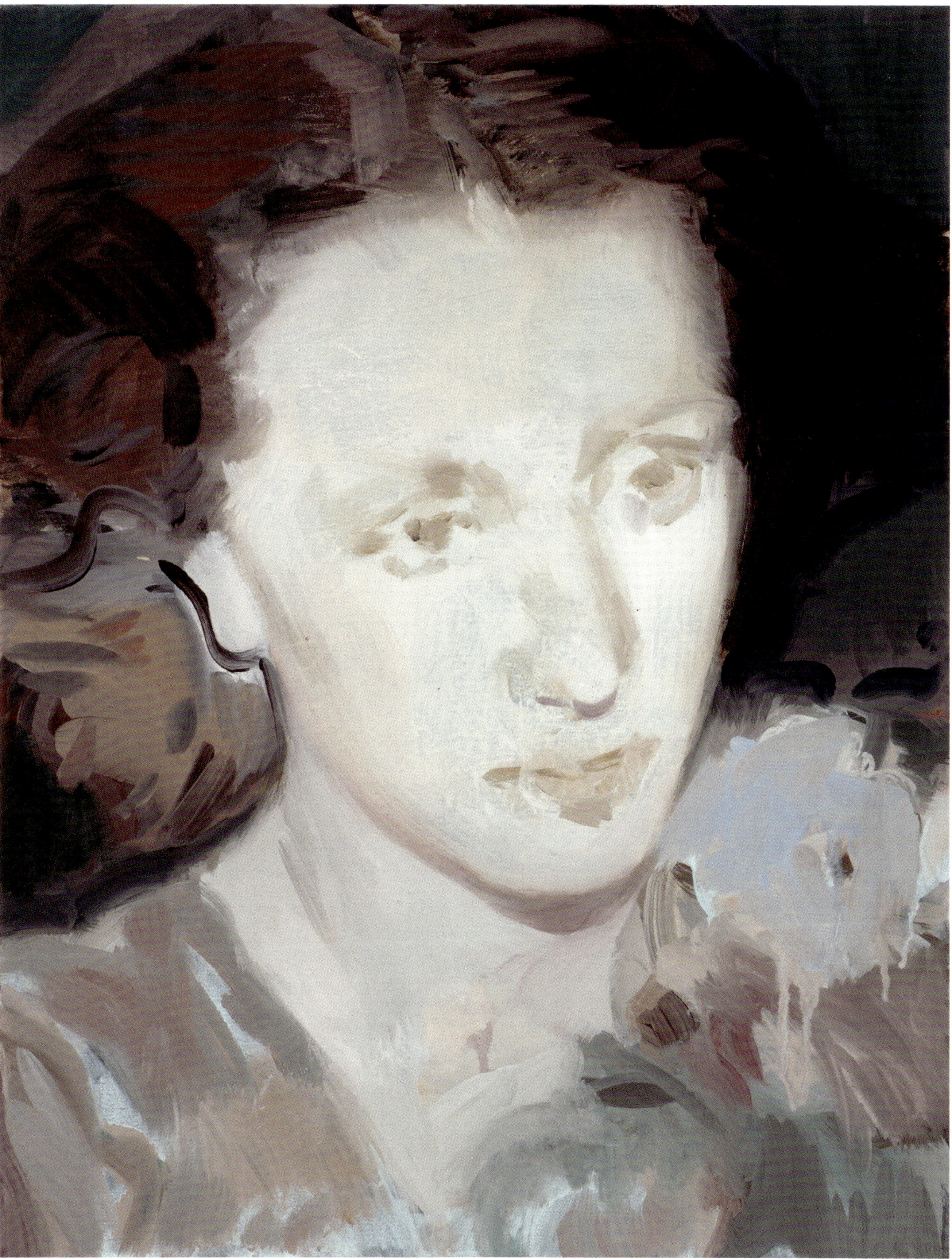

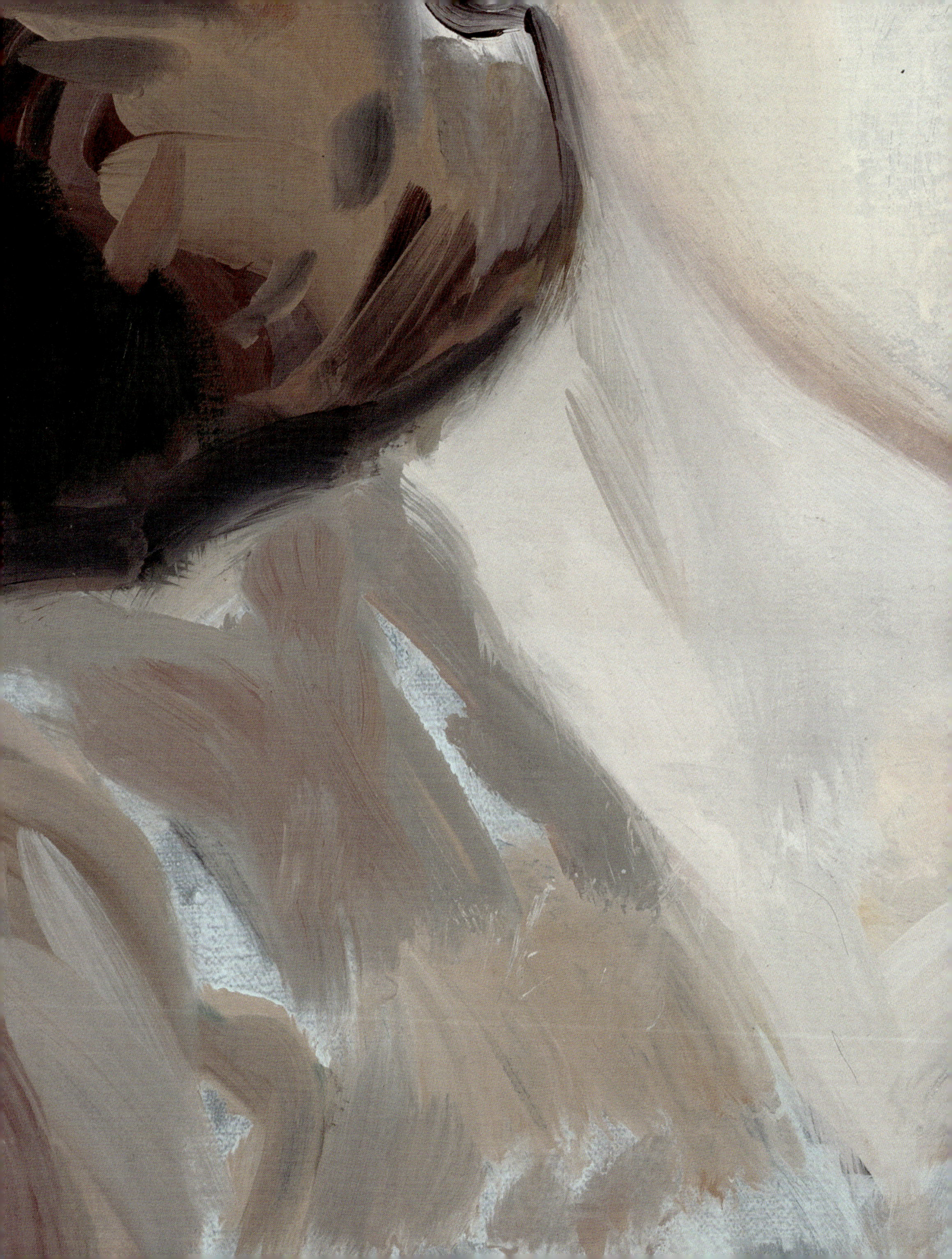

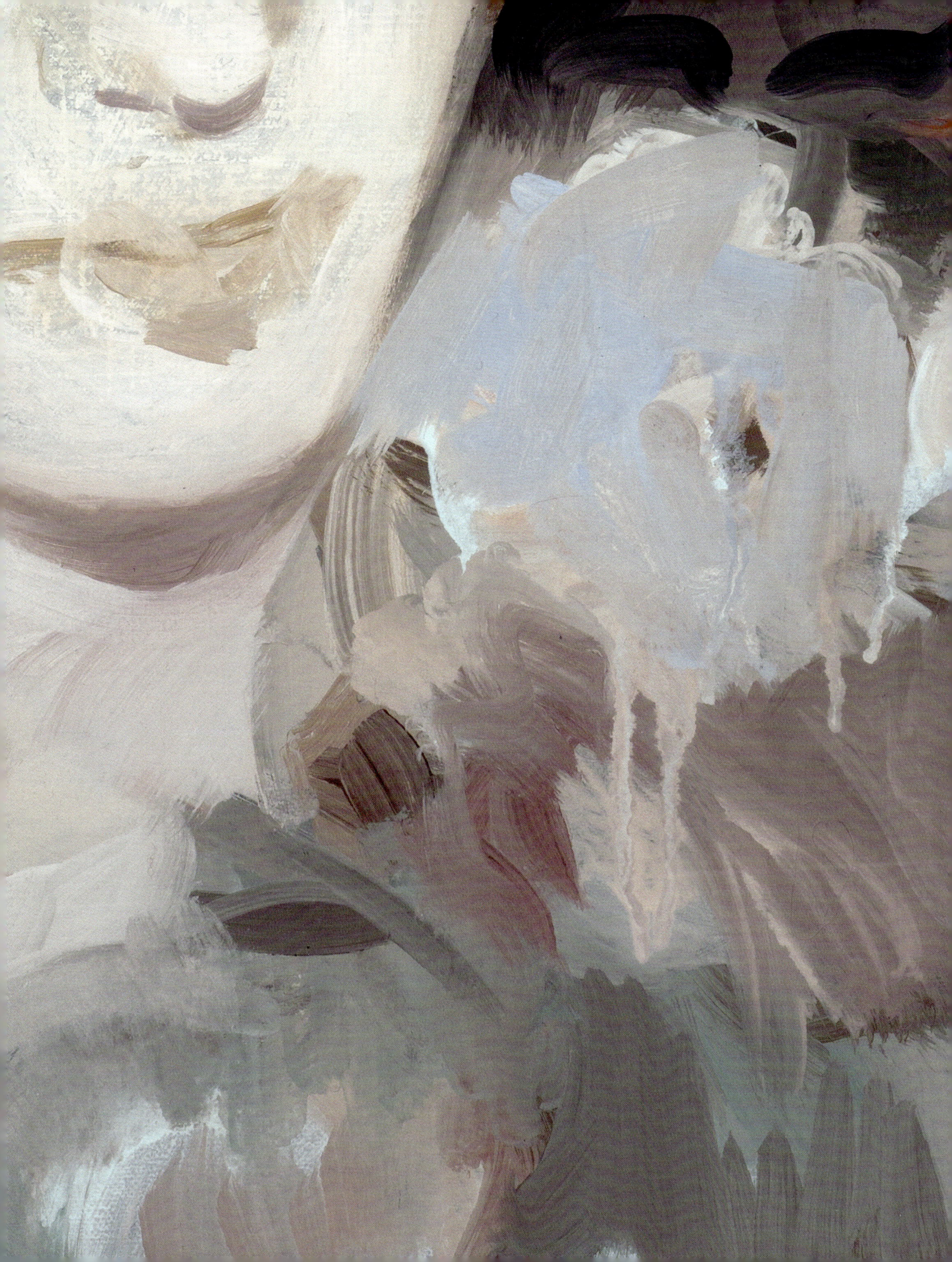

Freya Douglas-Morris

The Artist's View, 2025
Oil on canvas
185 × 165 cm
72⅞ × 65 in.

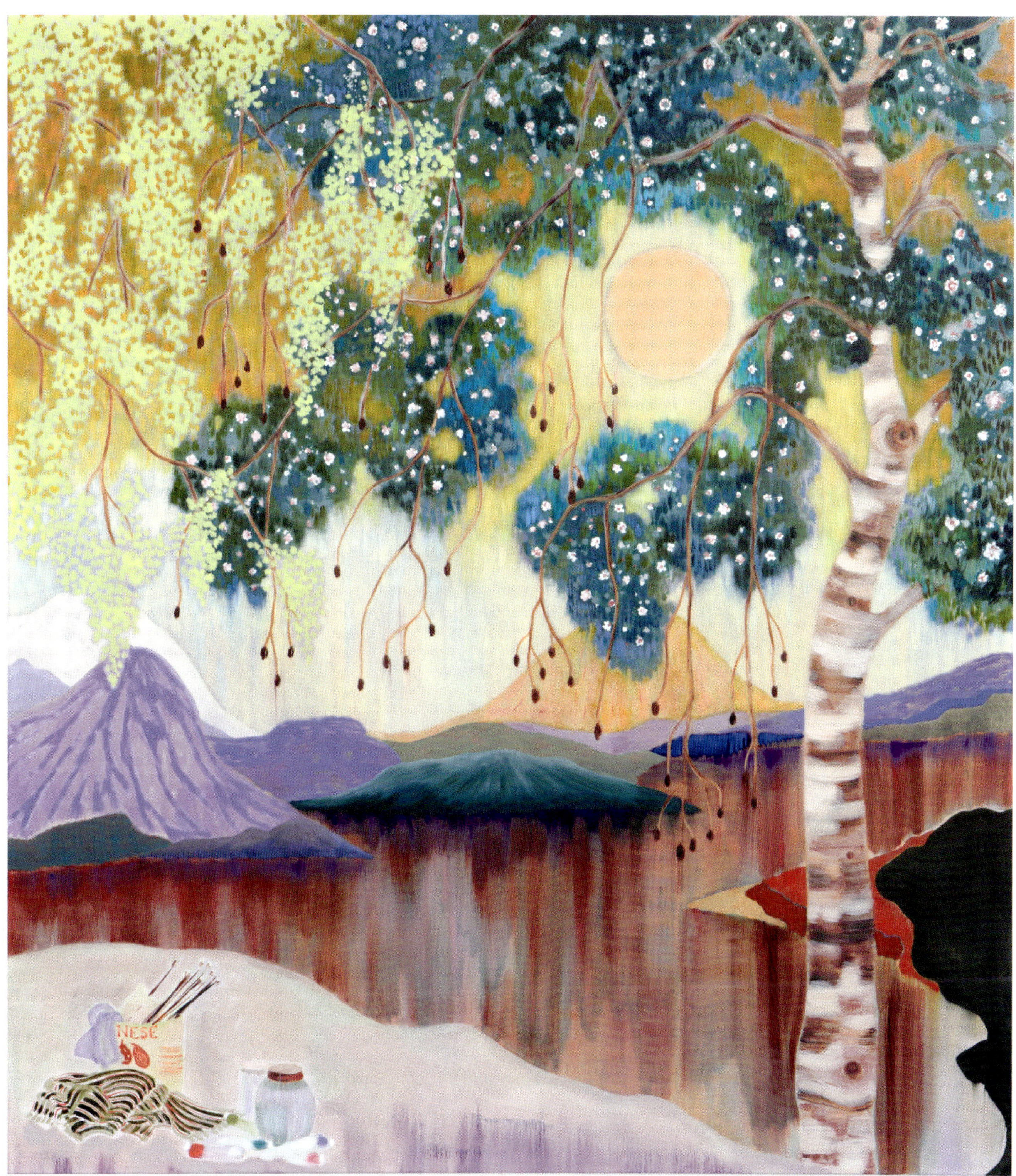
NESE

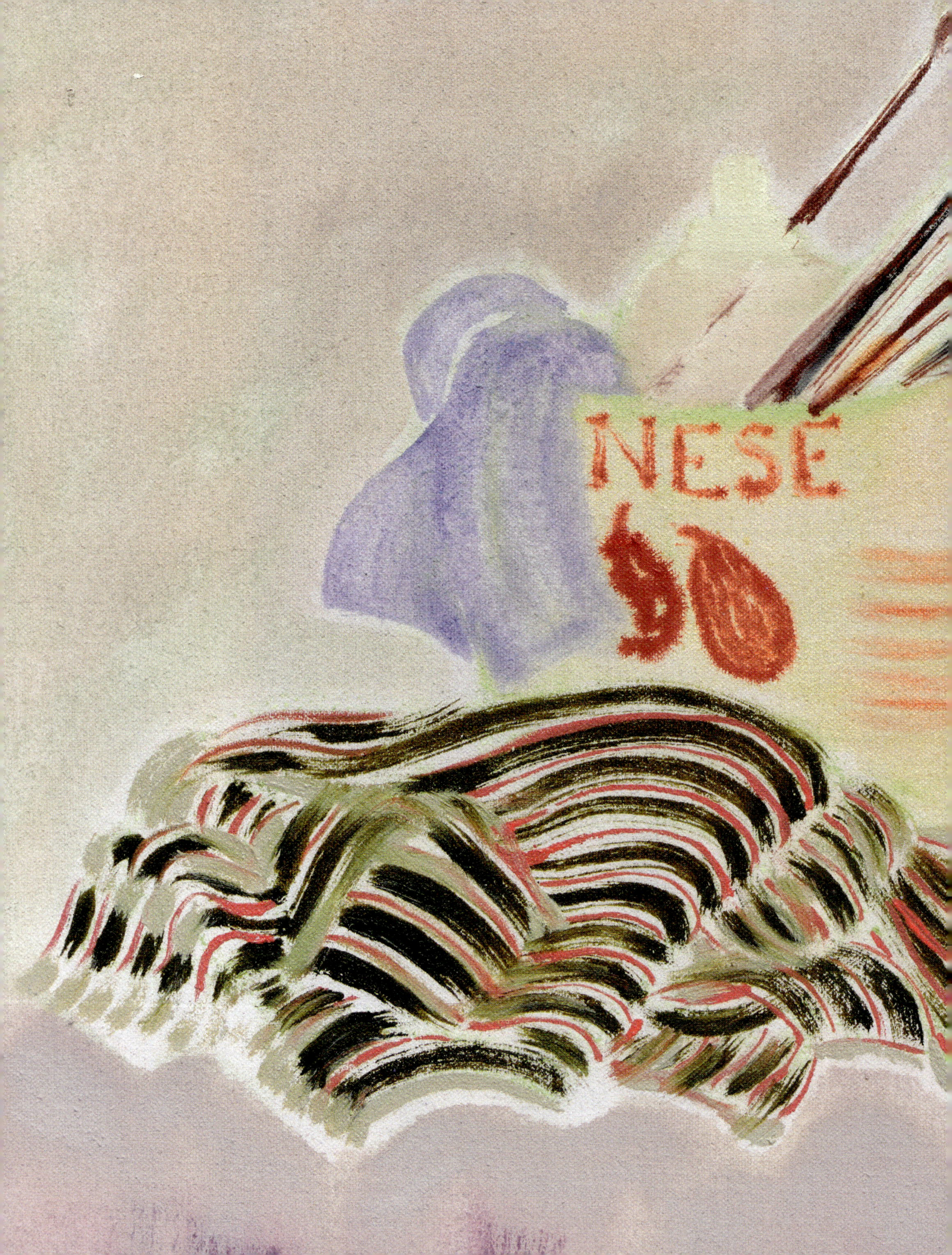
NESE

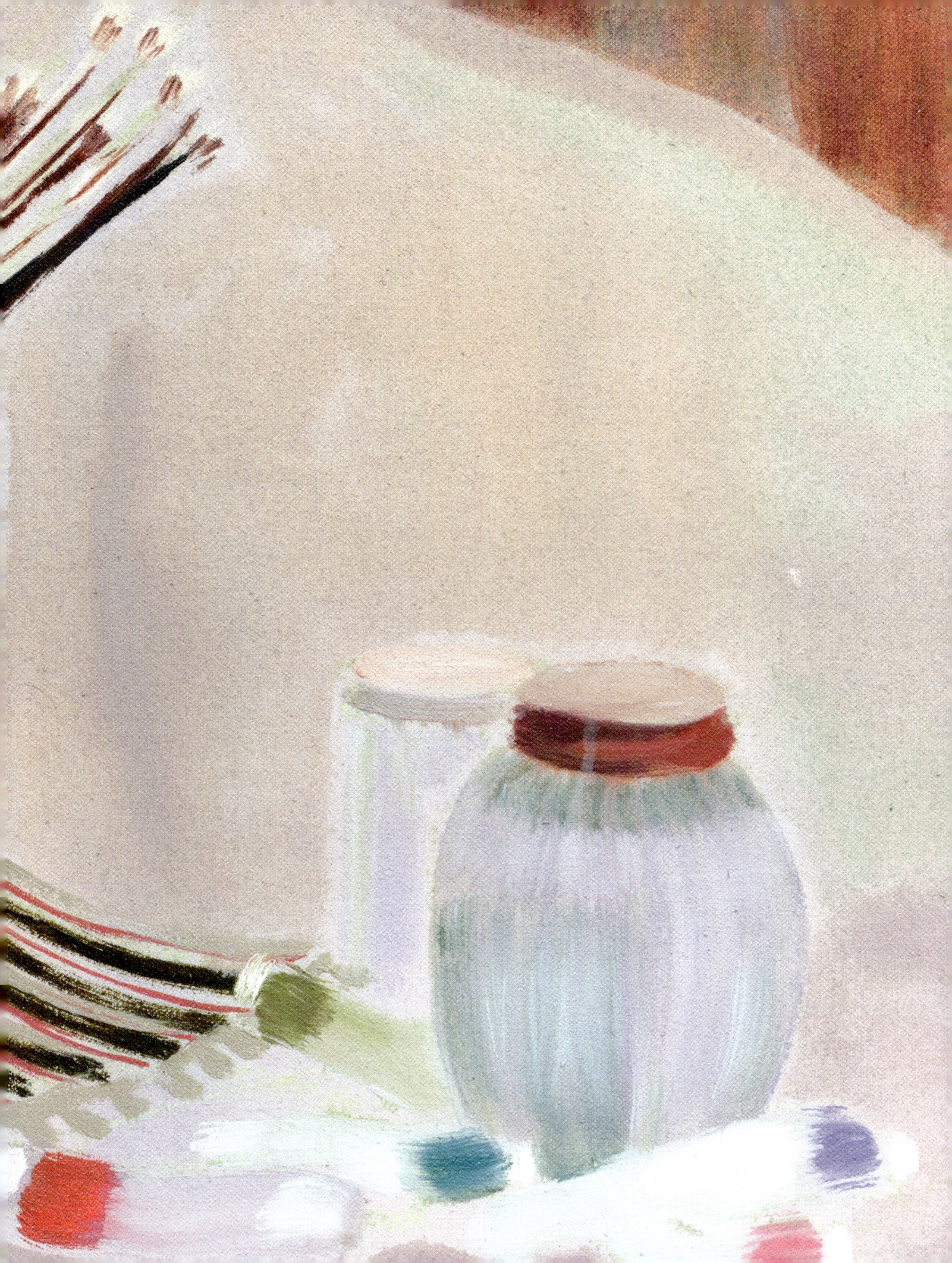

Anna Freeman Bentley

Garden tableau, 2025
Oil on canvas
140 × 187 cm
55⅛ × 73⅝ in.

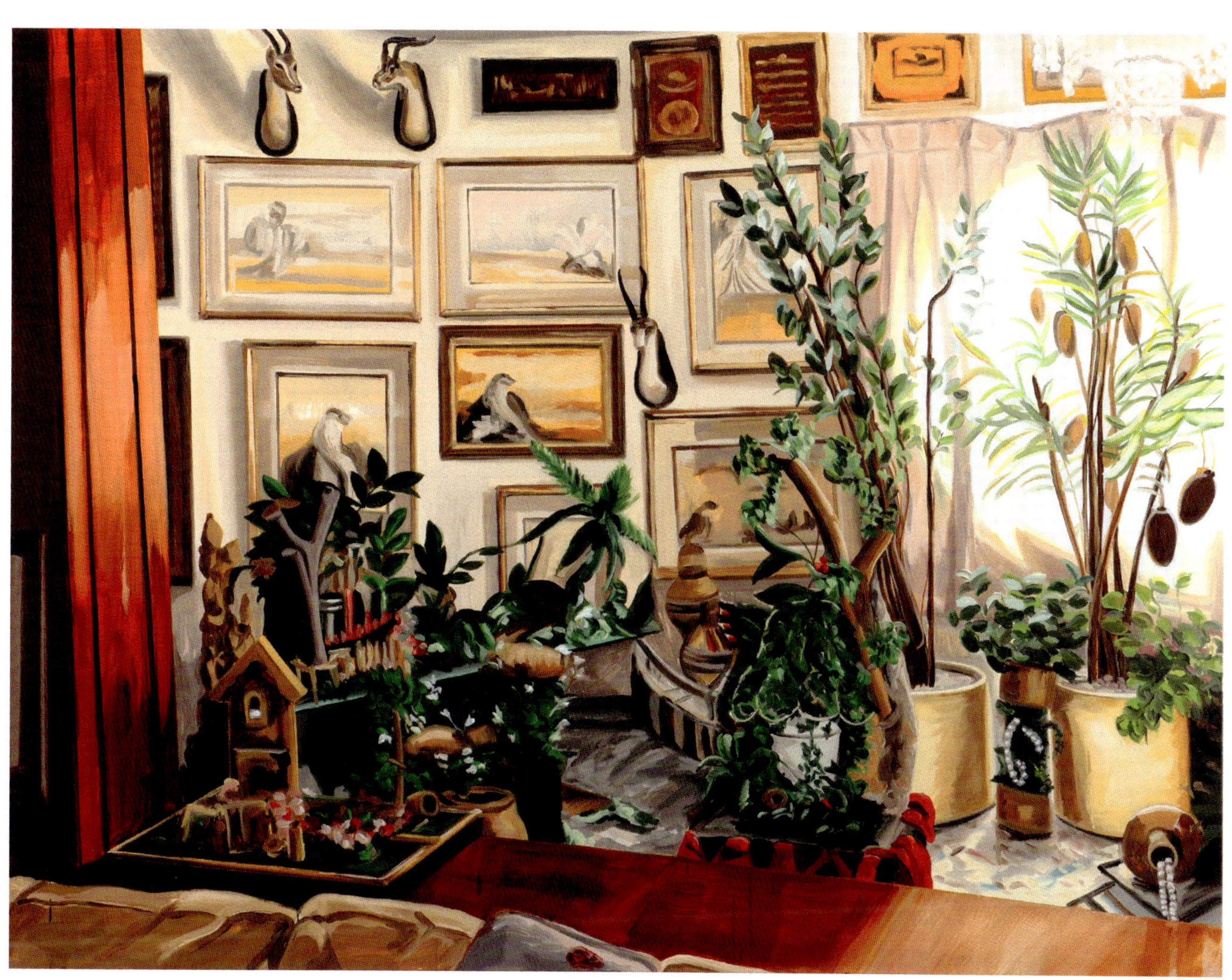

Nick Goss

Paradiso Island Approach, 2025
Distemper, oil and silk screen
on linen
150 × 130 cm
59 × 51⅛ in.

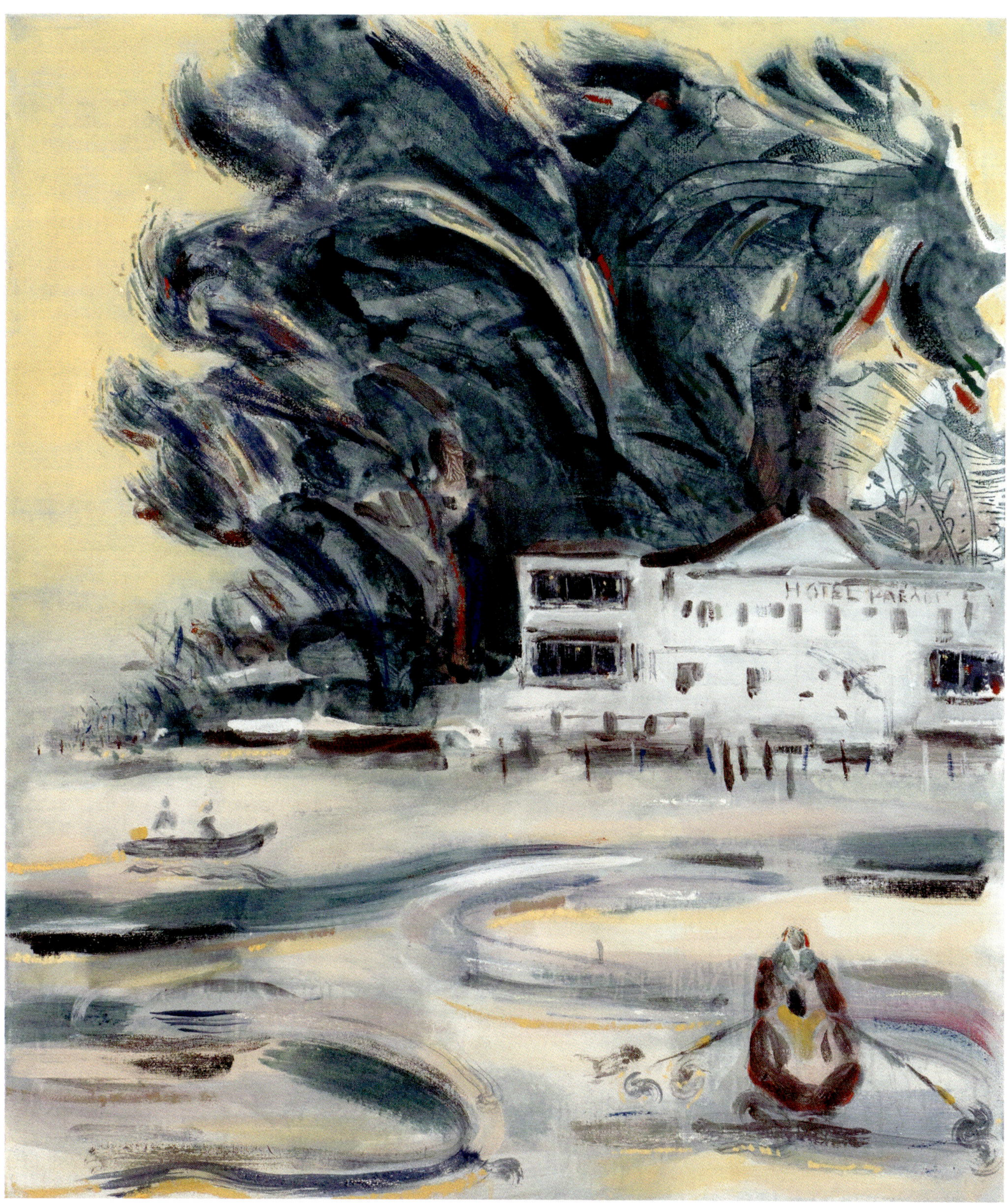

Sunyoung Hwang

Flash On, 2025
Oil on canvas
153 × 183 cm
60¼ × 72 in.

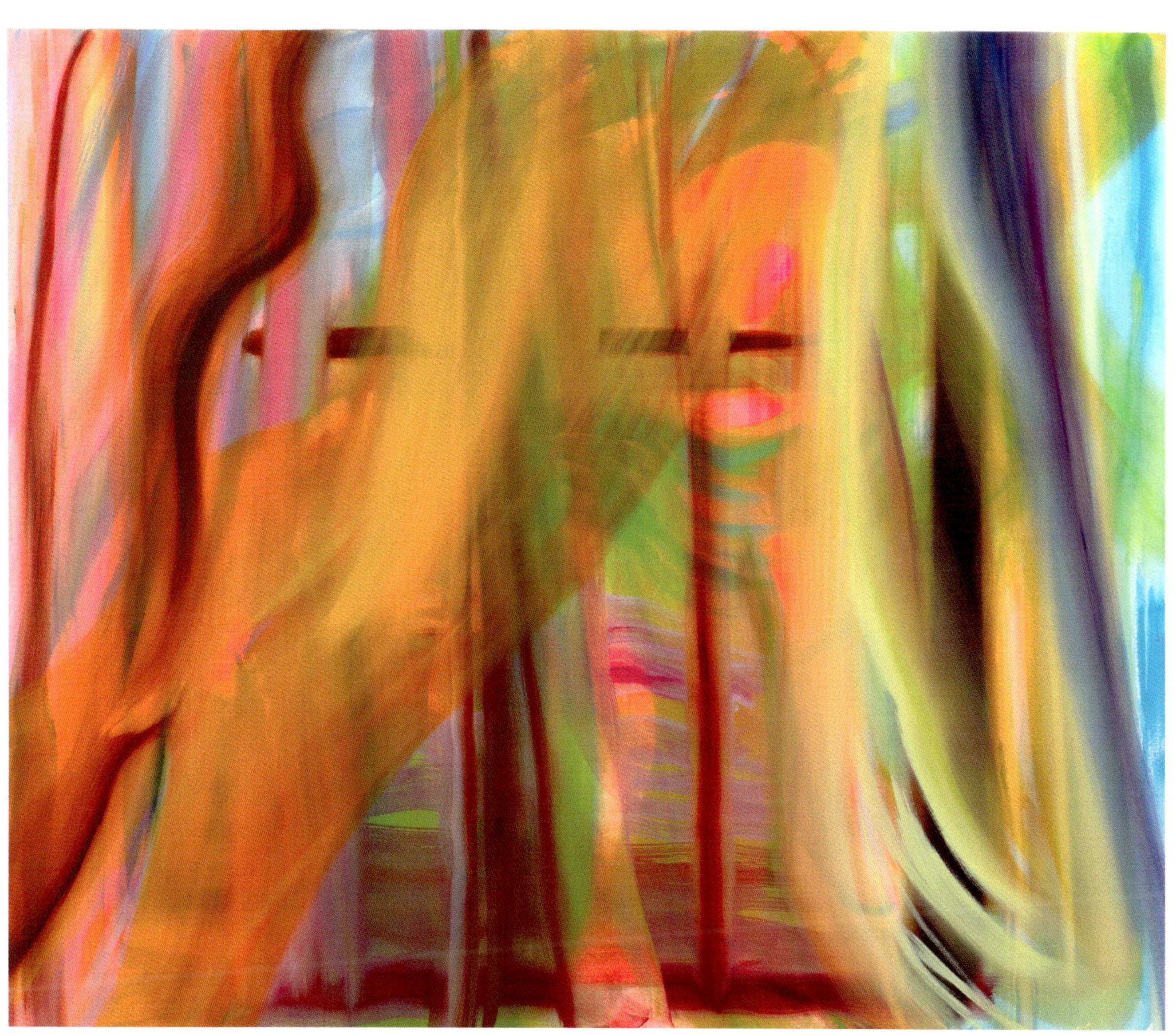

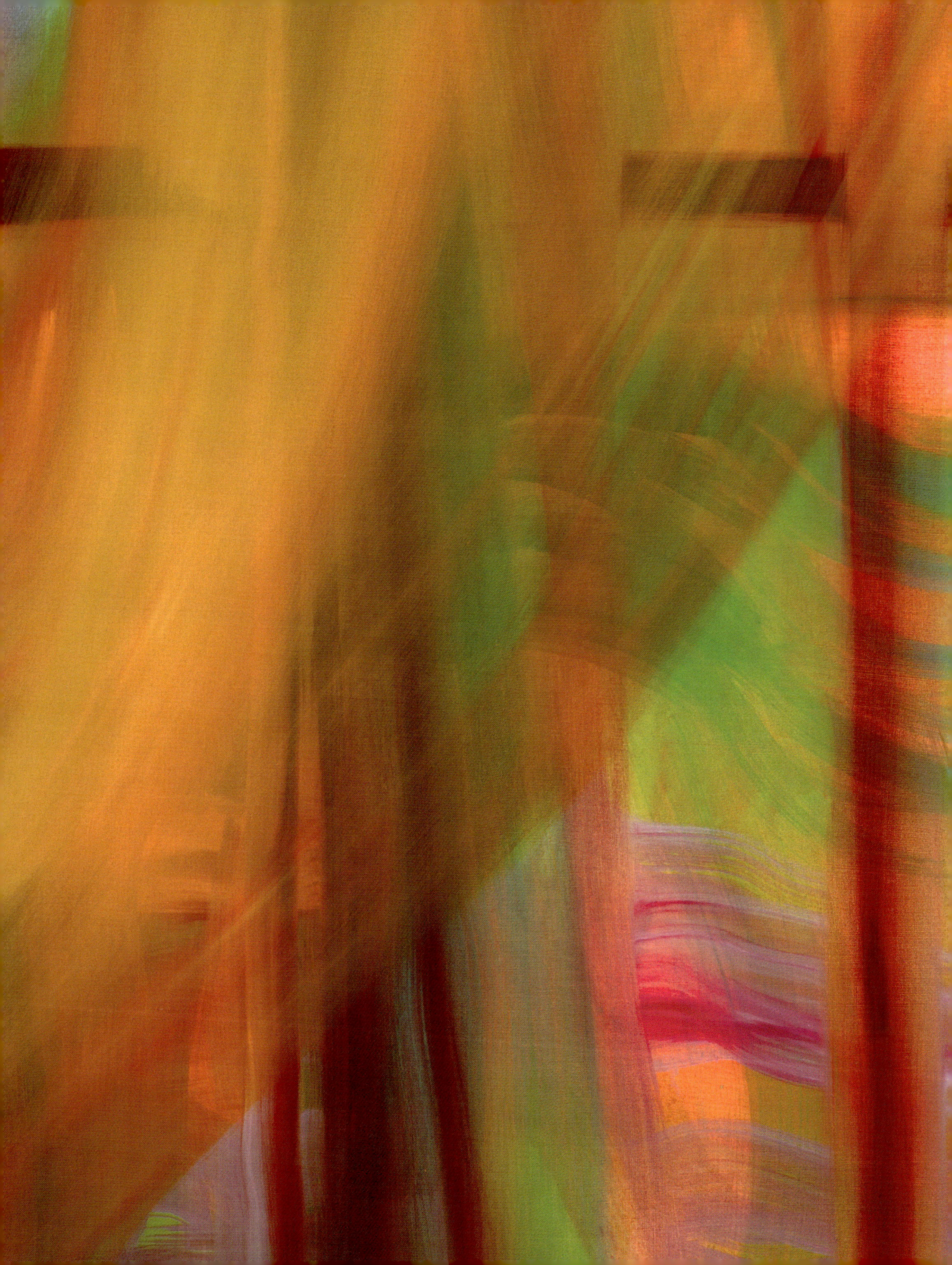

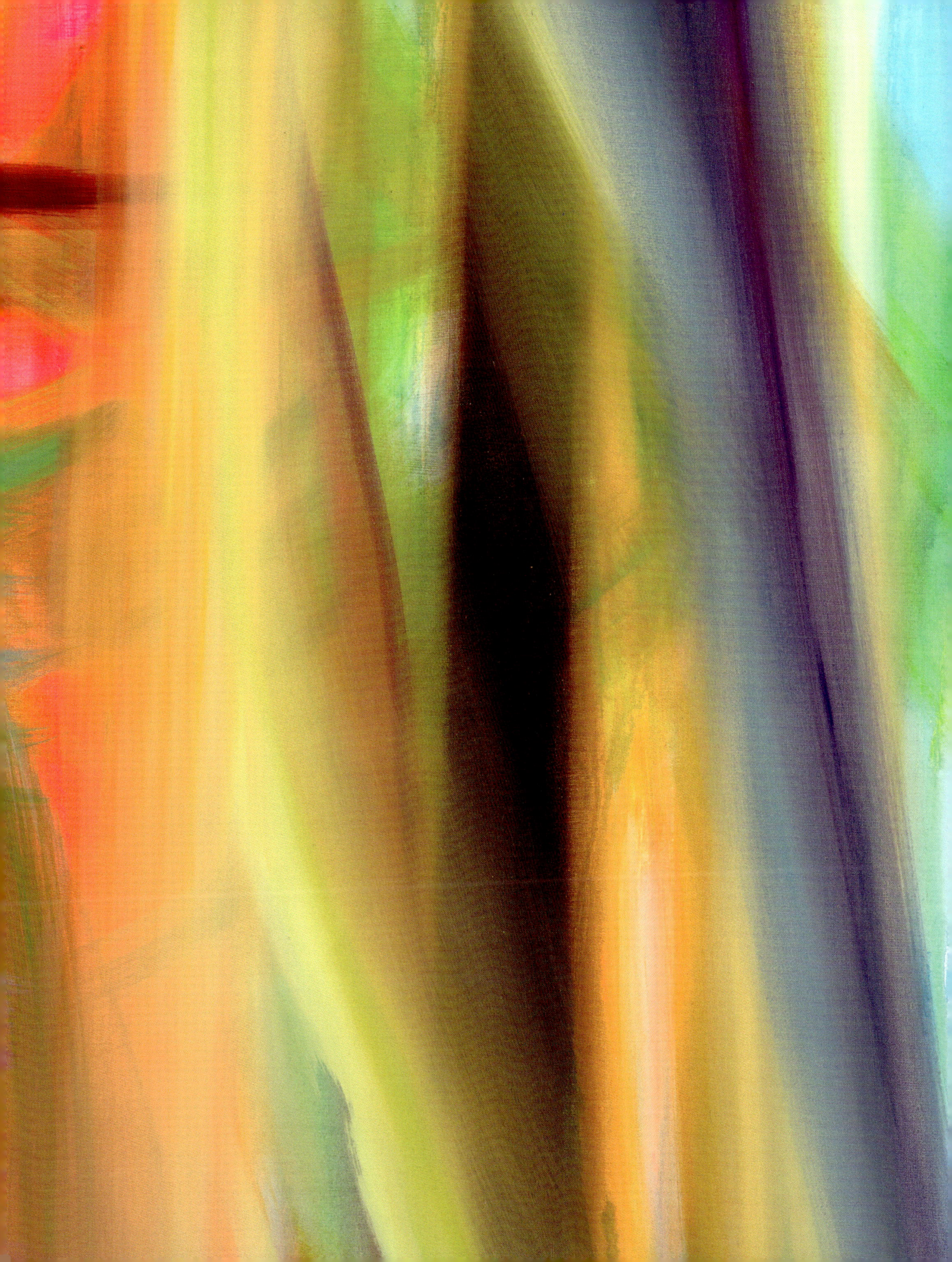

Minami Kobayashi

*The copper hair and cherry blossom
trees along the river*, 2025
Oil on canvas
80 × 130 cm
31½ x 51⅛ in.

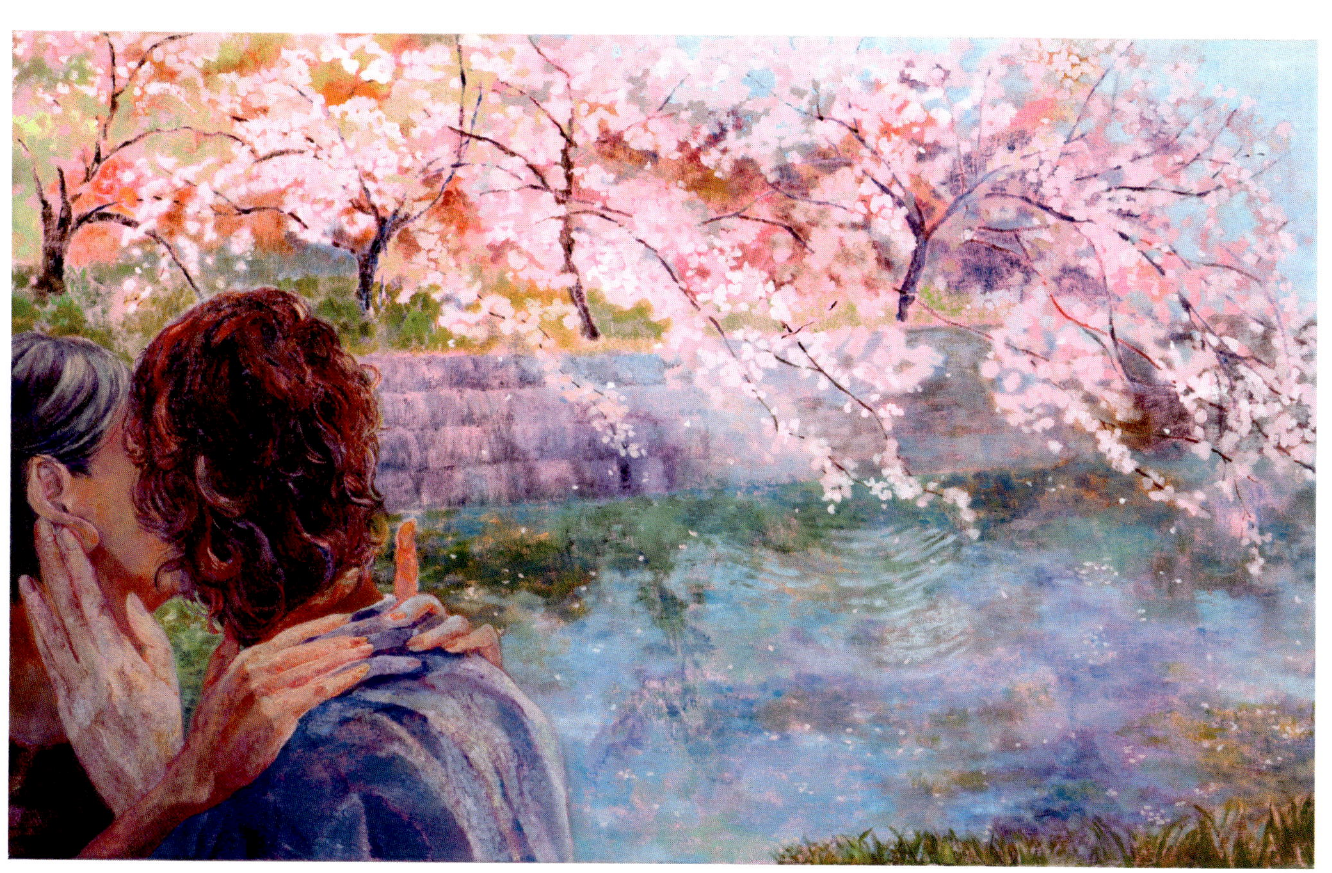

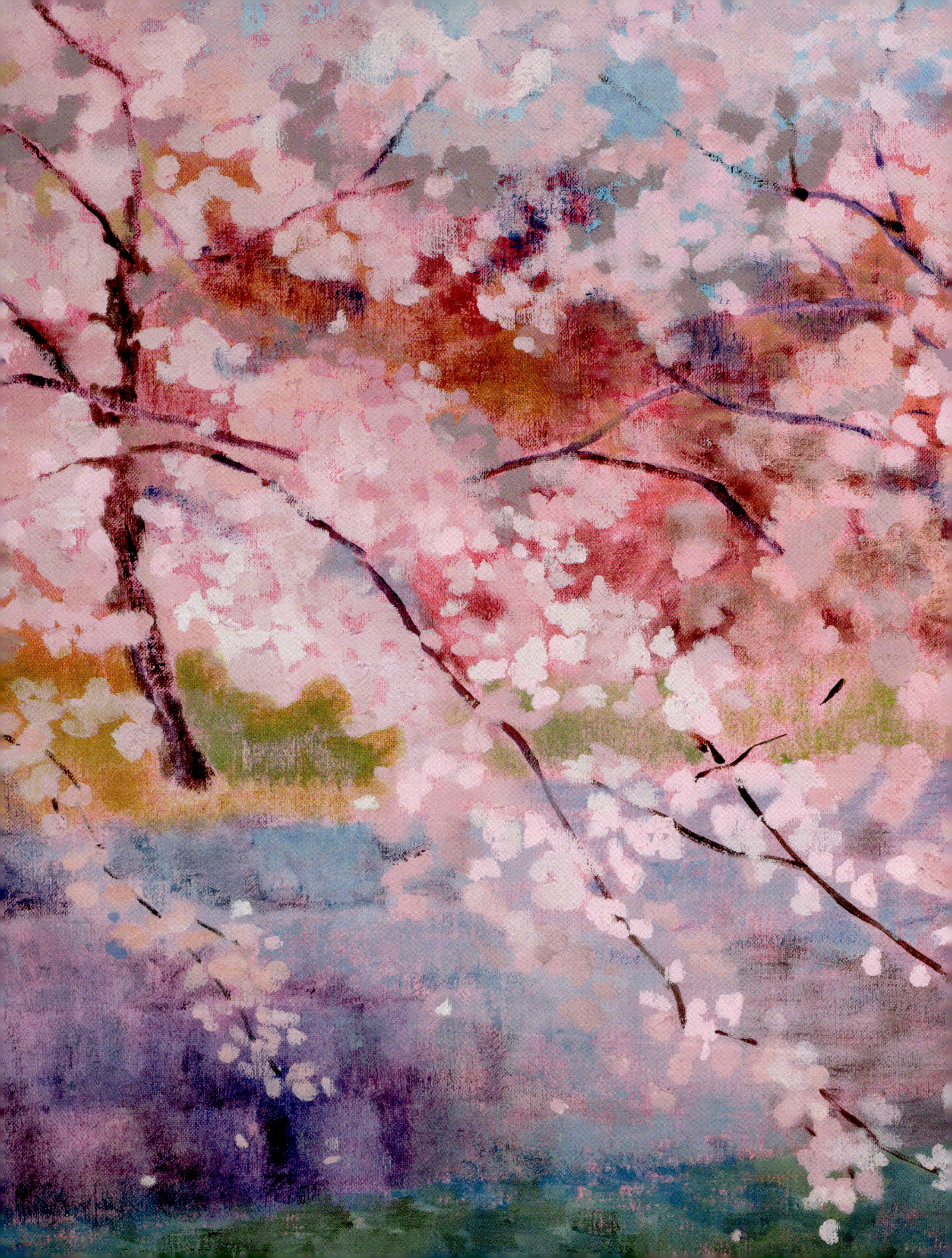

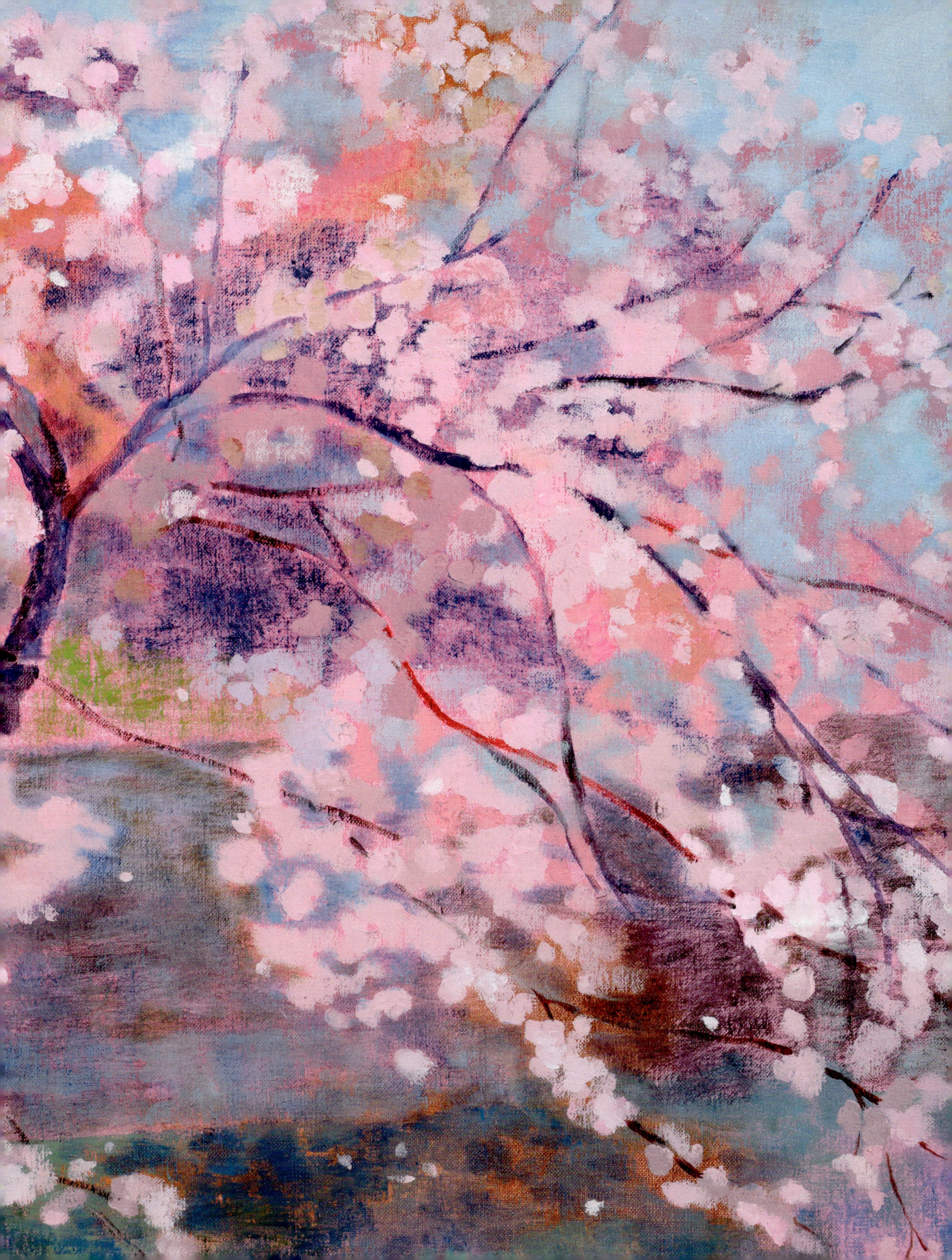

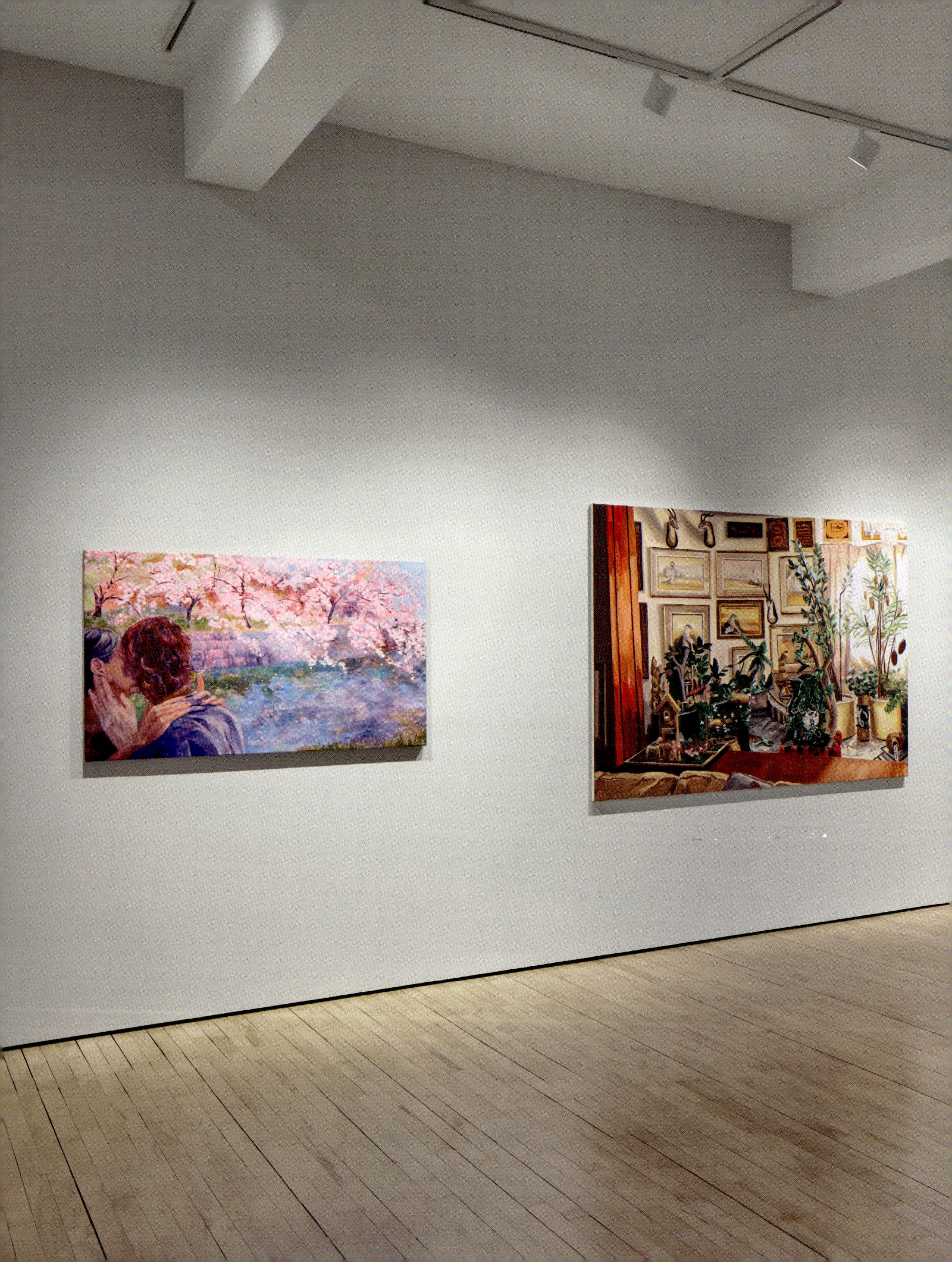

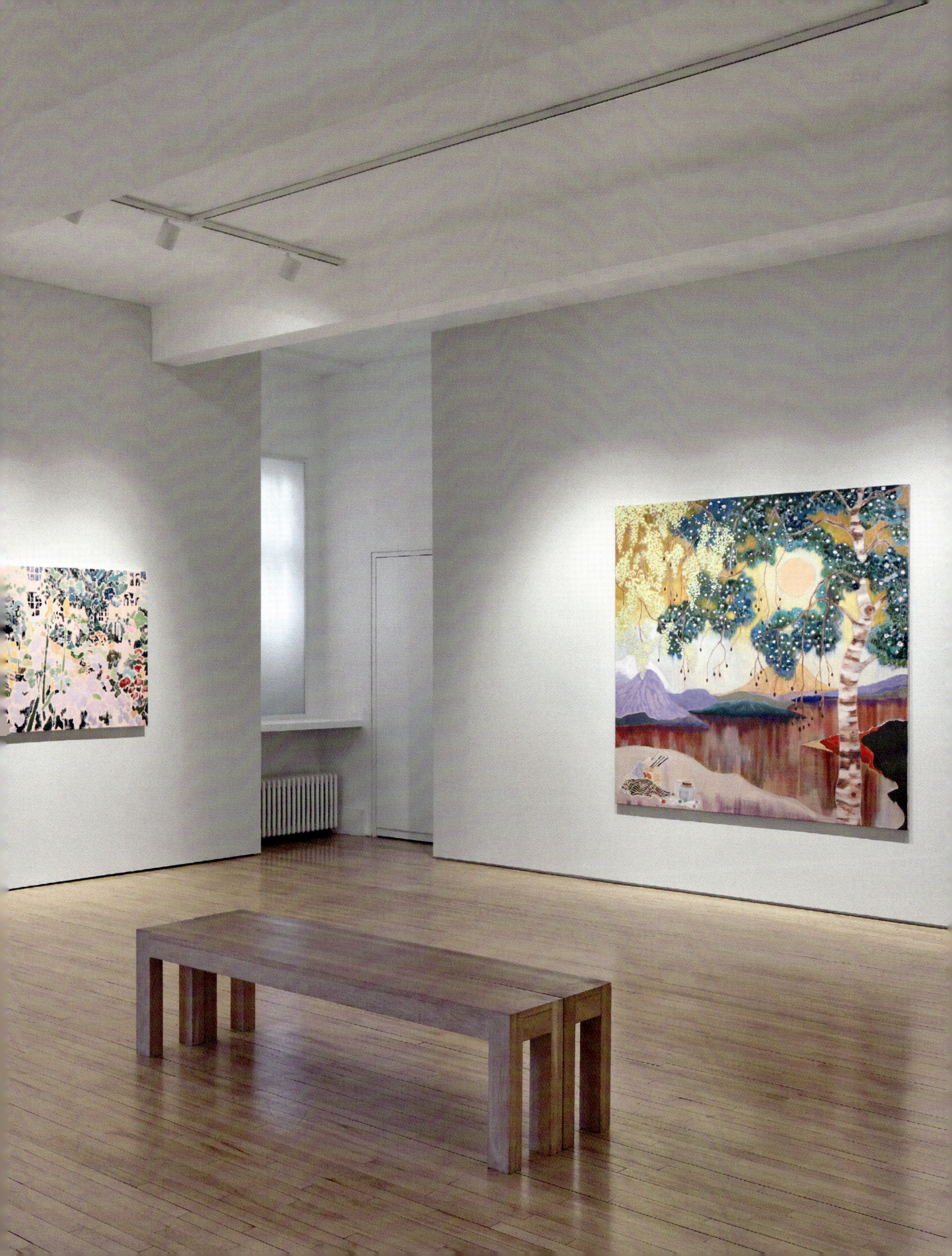

Matthew Krishanu

Boy Swimming (Wave), 2025
Oil and acrylic on board
46 × 36 cm
18⅛ × 14⅛ in.

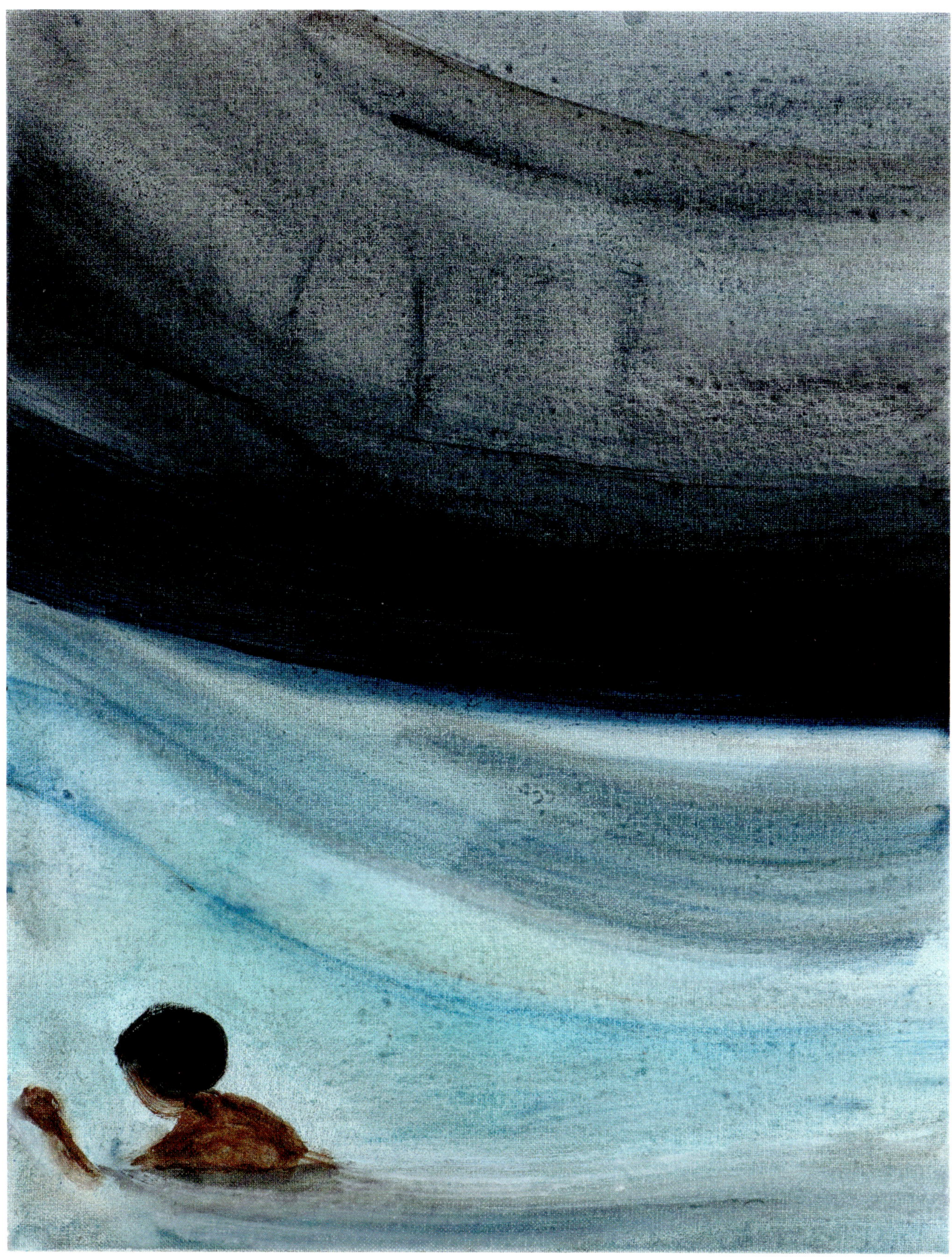

Des Lawrence

Obituary Painting: David Hessayon,
2025
Oil on board
44 × 62 cm
17³⁄₈ × 24³⁄₈ in.

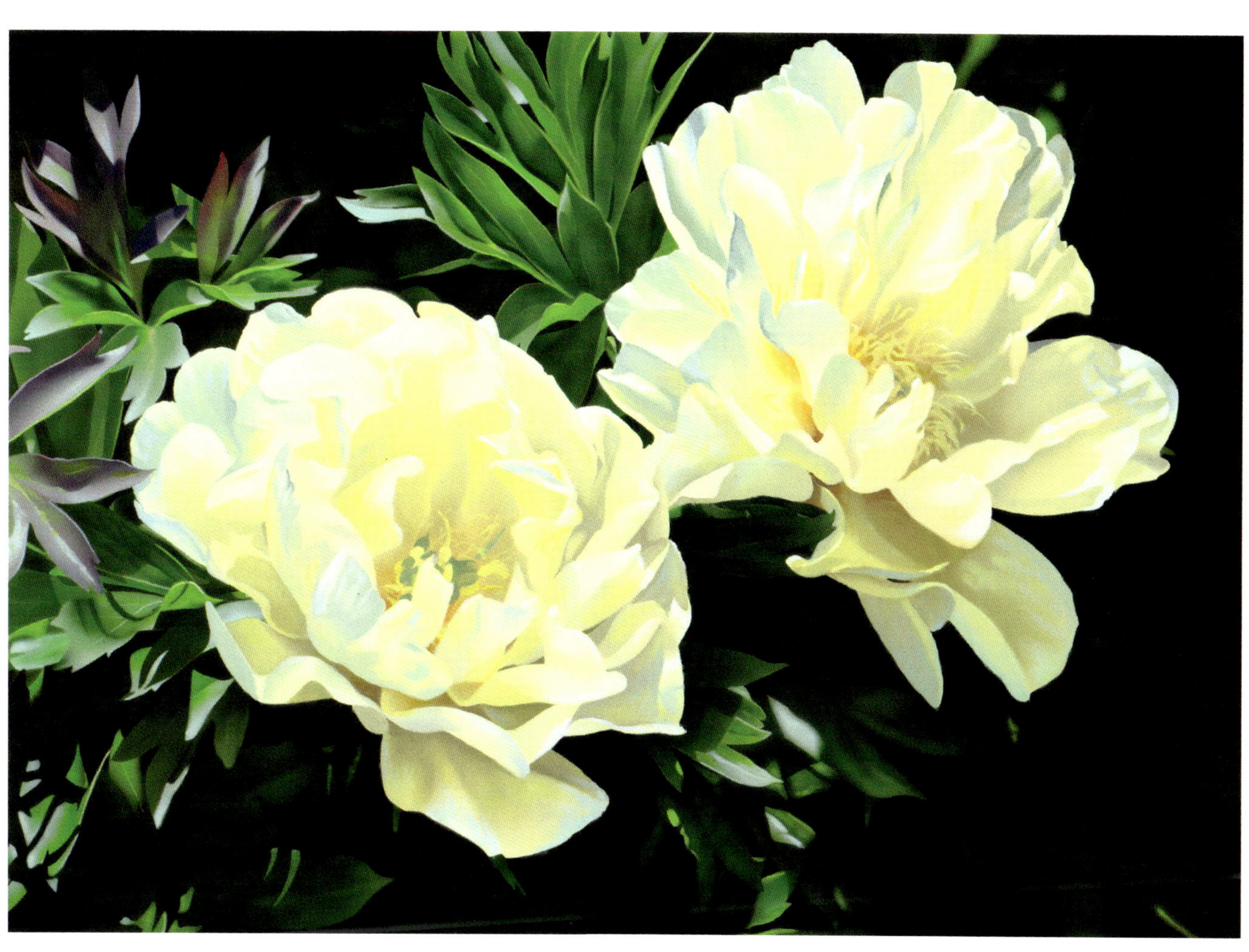

Jessie Makinson

Some Sort of Commotion, 2025
Oil on linen
120.5 × 100.5 cm
47½ × 39⅝ in.

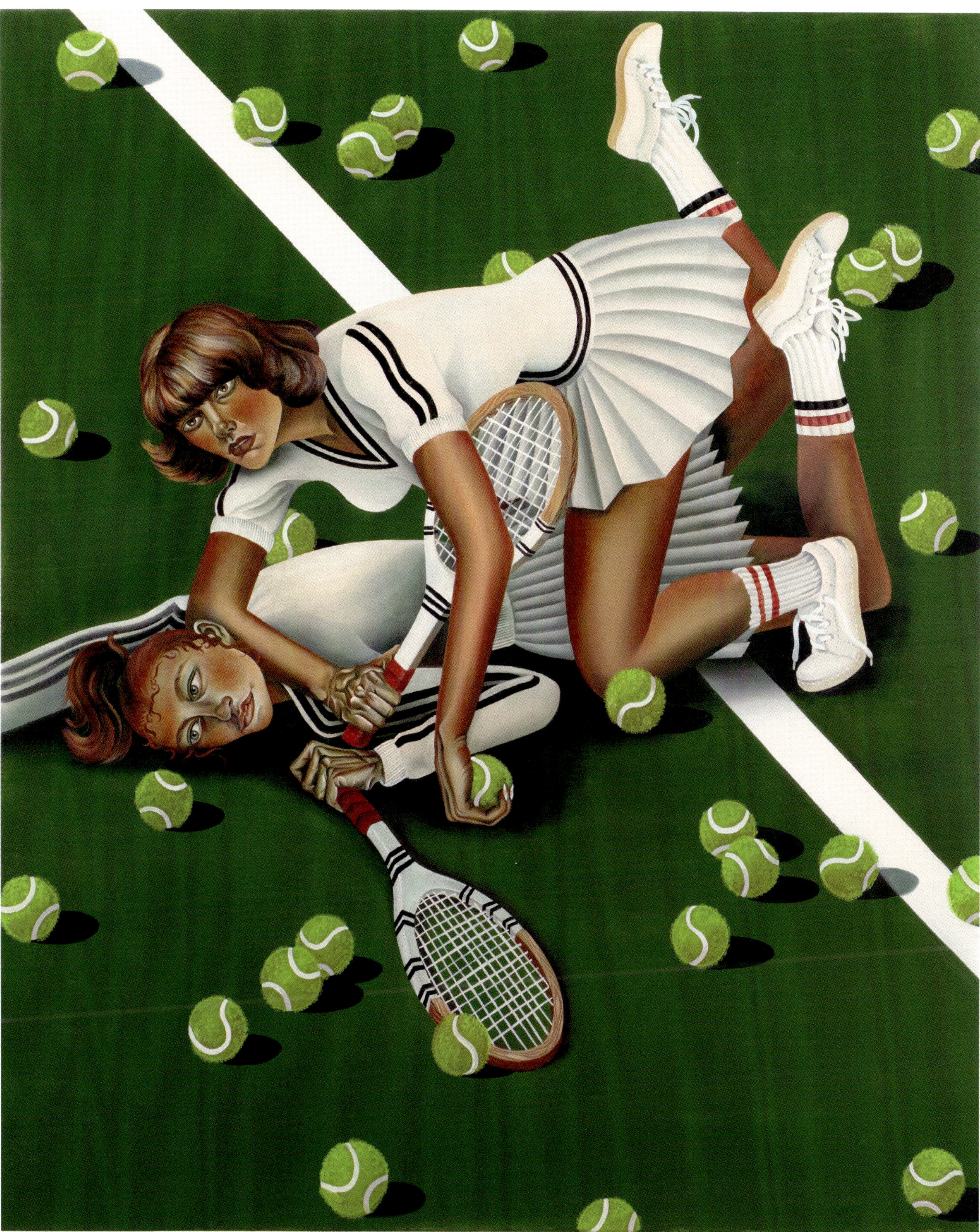

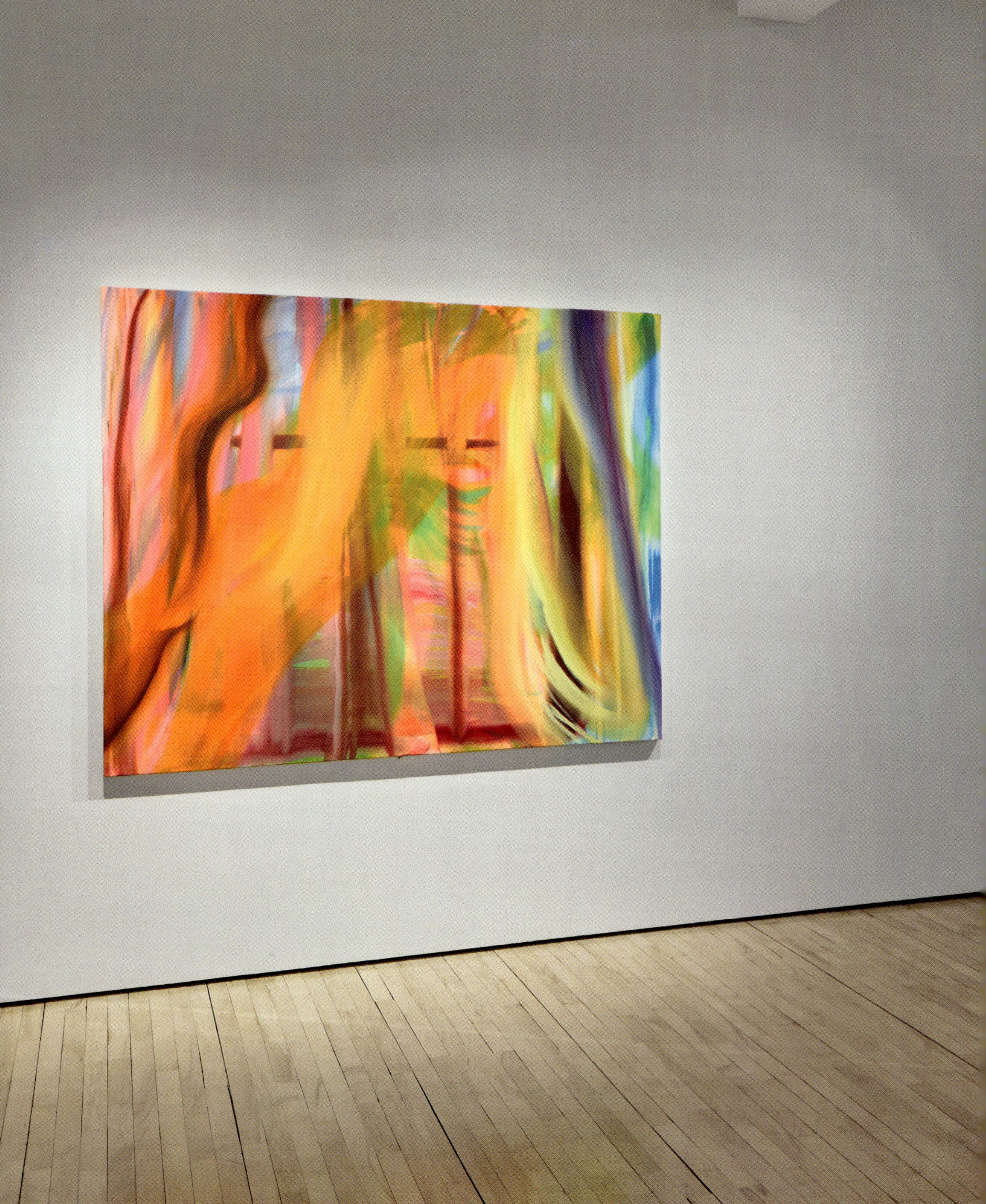

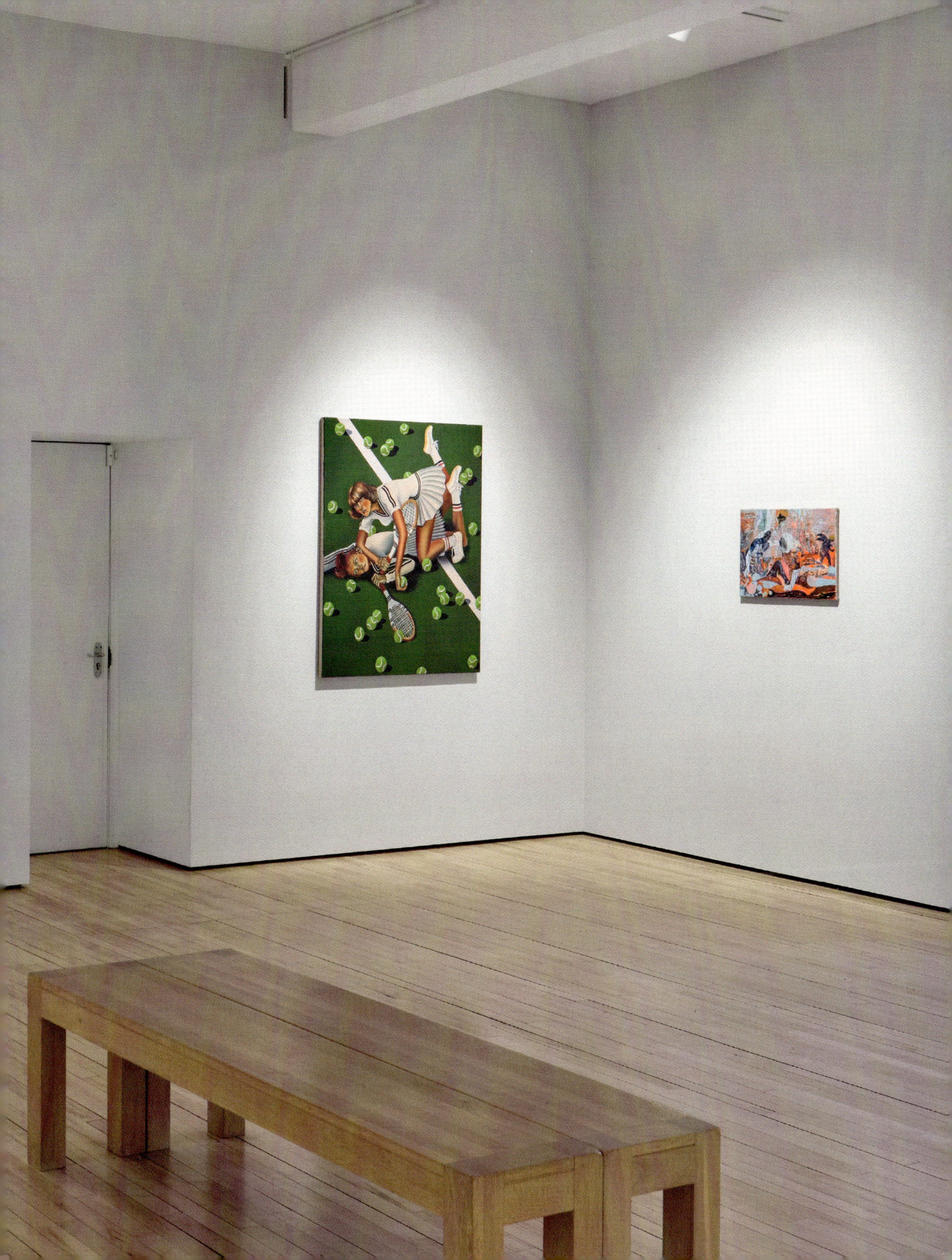

Kathryn Maple

Inside Out, 2025
Watercolour on paper
75 × 108 cm
29½ × 42½ in.

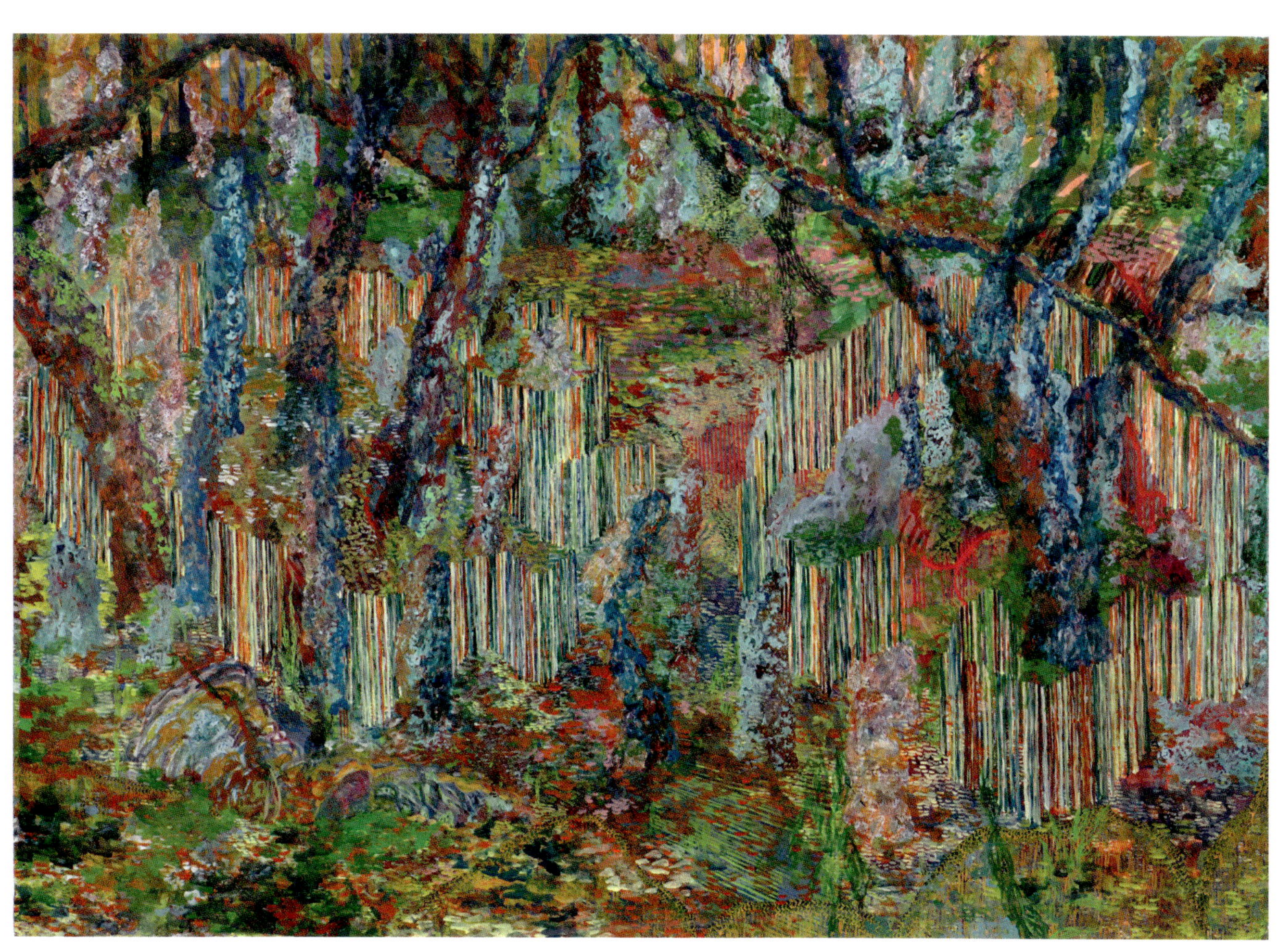

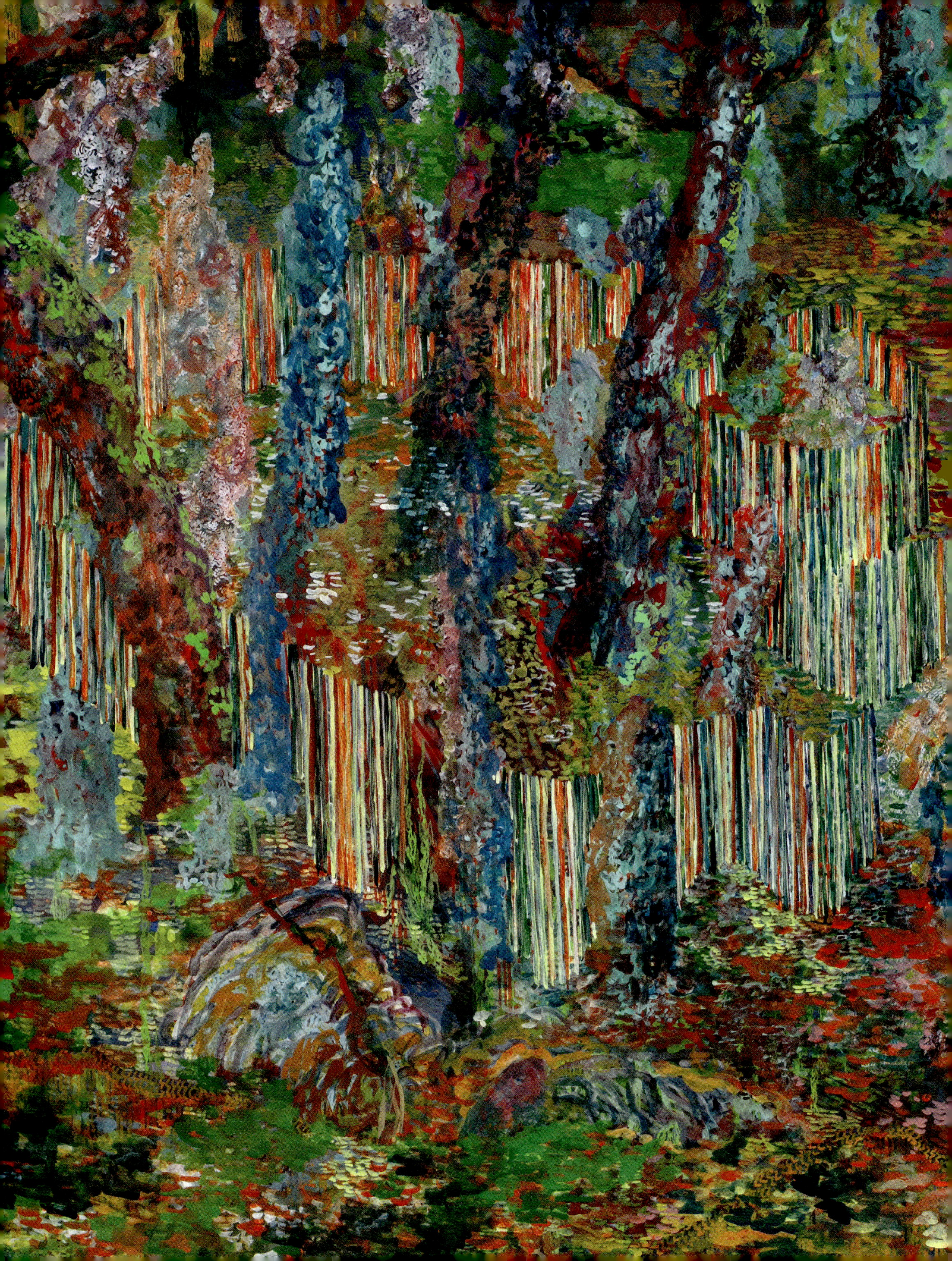

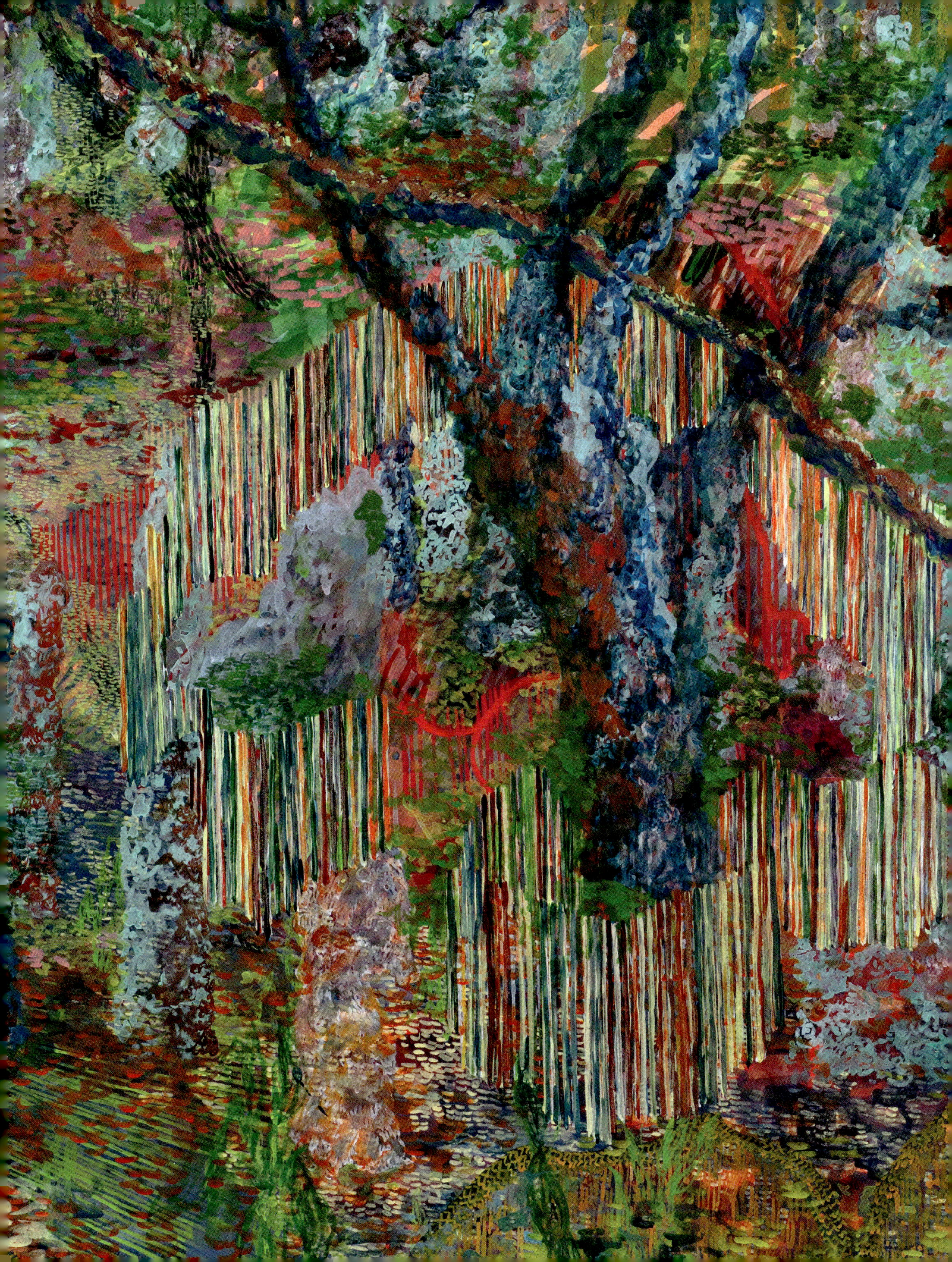

Barry McGlashan

*No Particular Night or
Morning*, 2025
Oil on panel
60 × 50.5 cm
23⅝ × 19⅞ in.

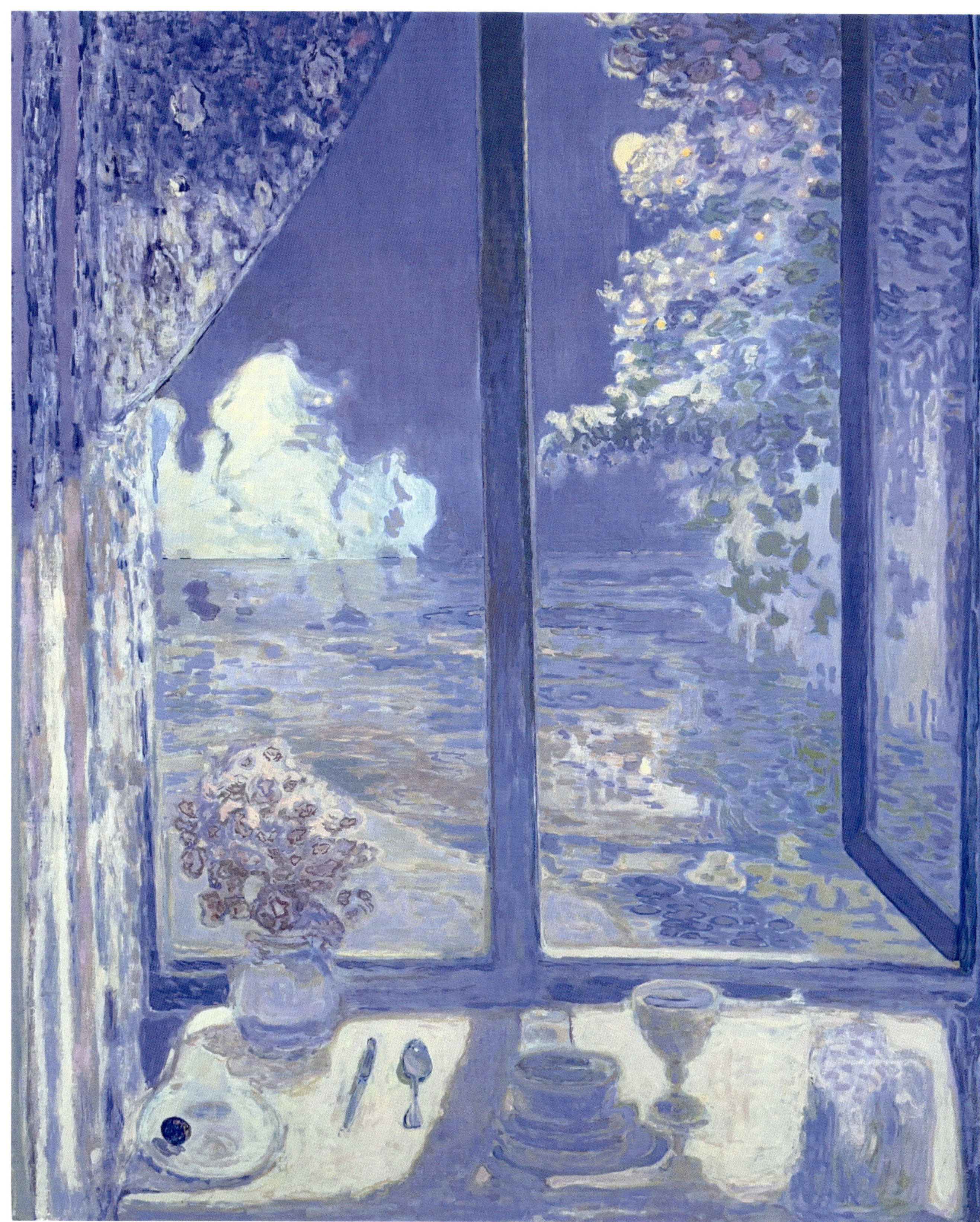

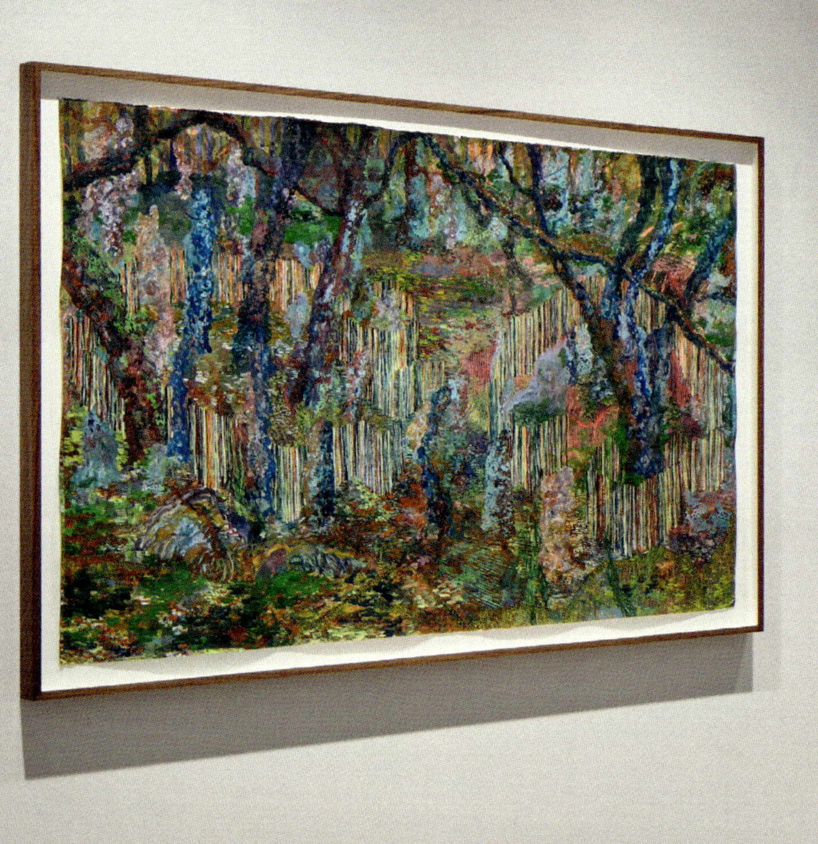
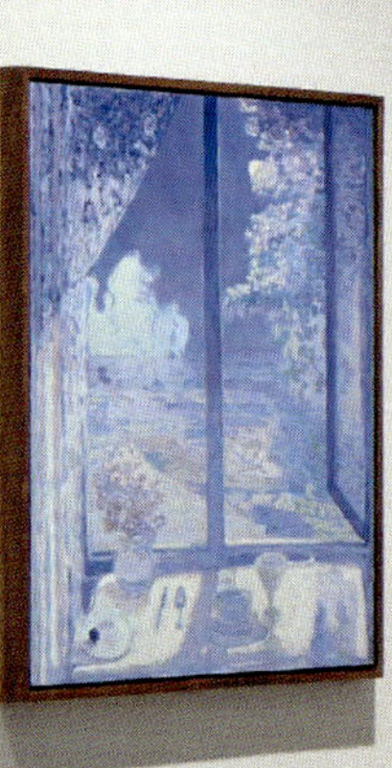

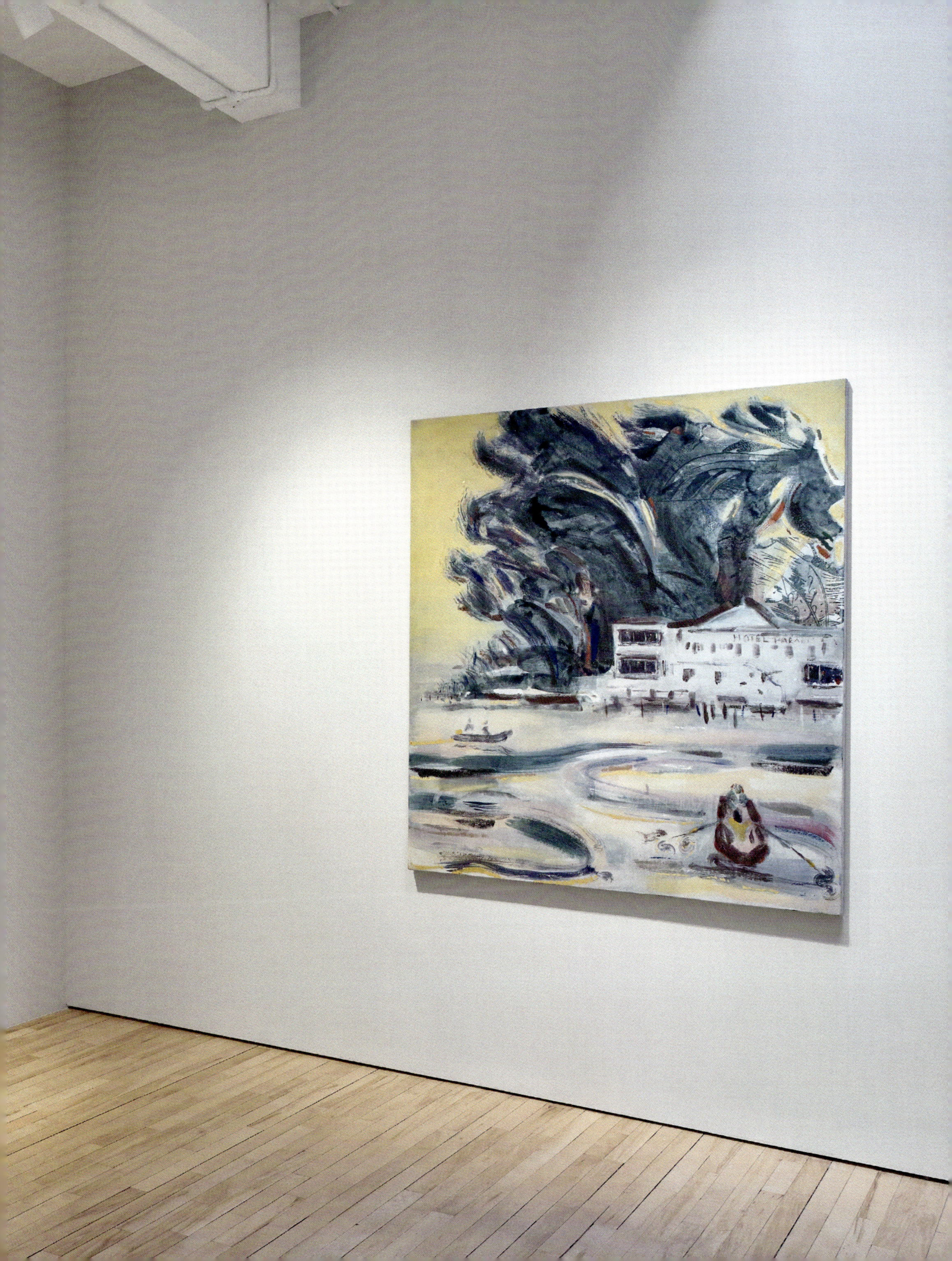
HOTEL PARADIS

Justin Mortimer

An Uncertain Afternoon, 2025
Oil on canvas
61 × 76 cm
24 × 29⅞ in.

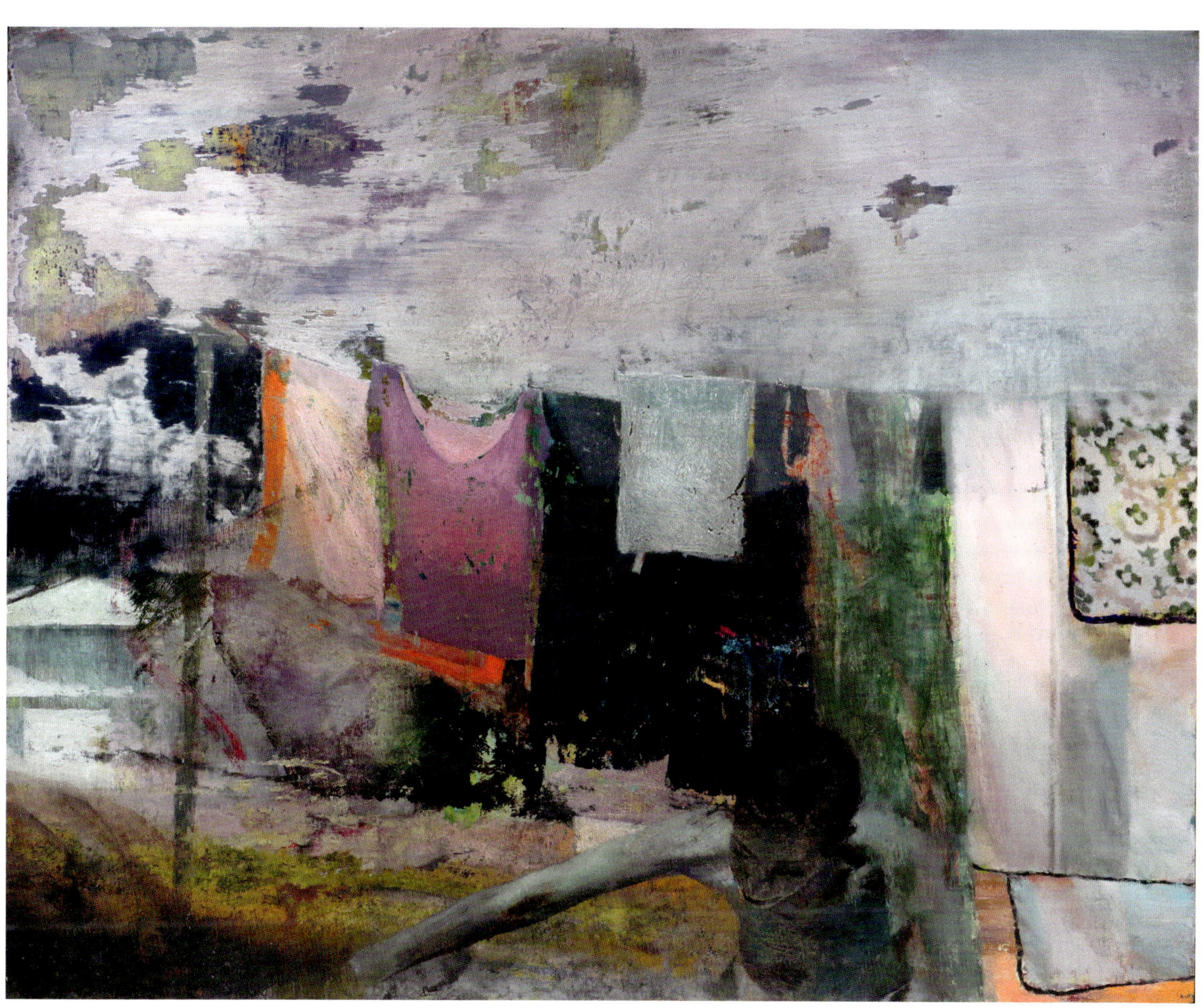

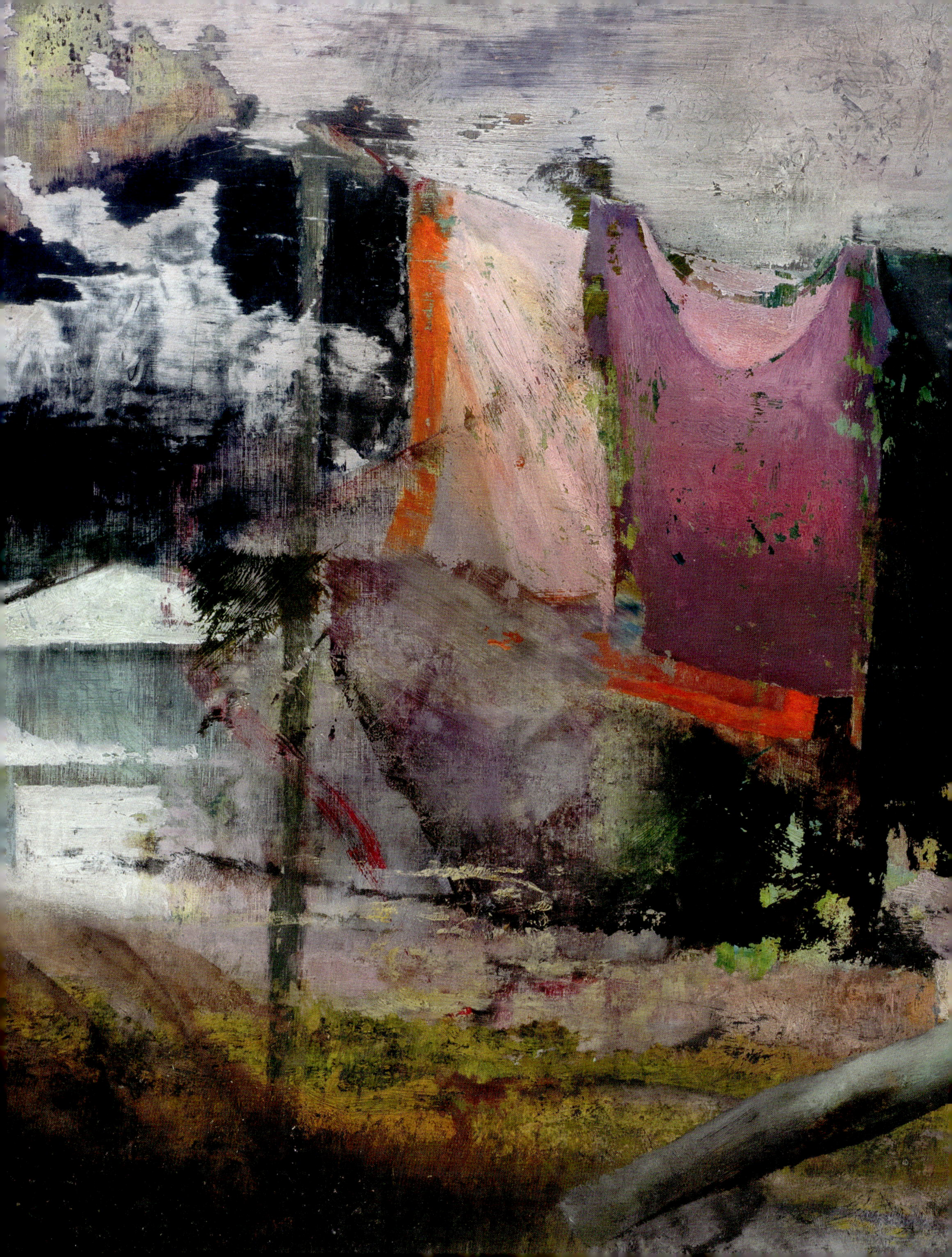

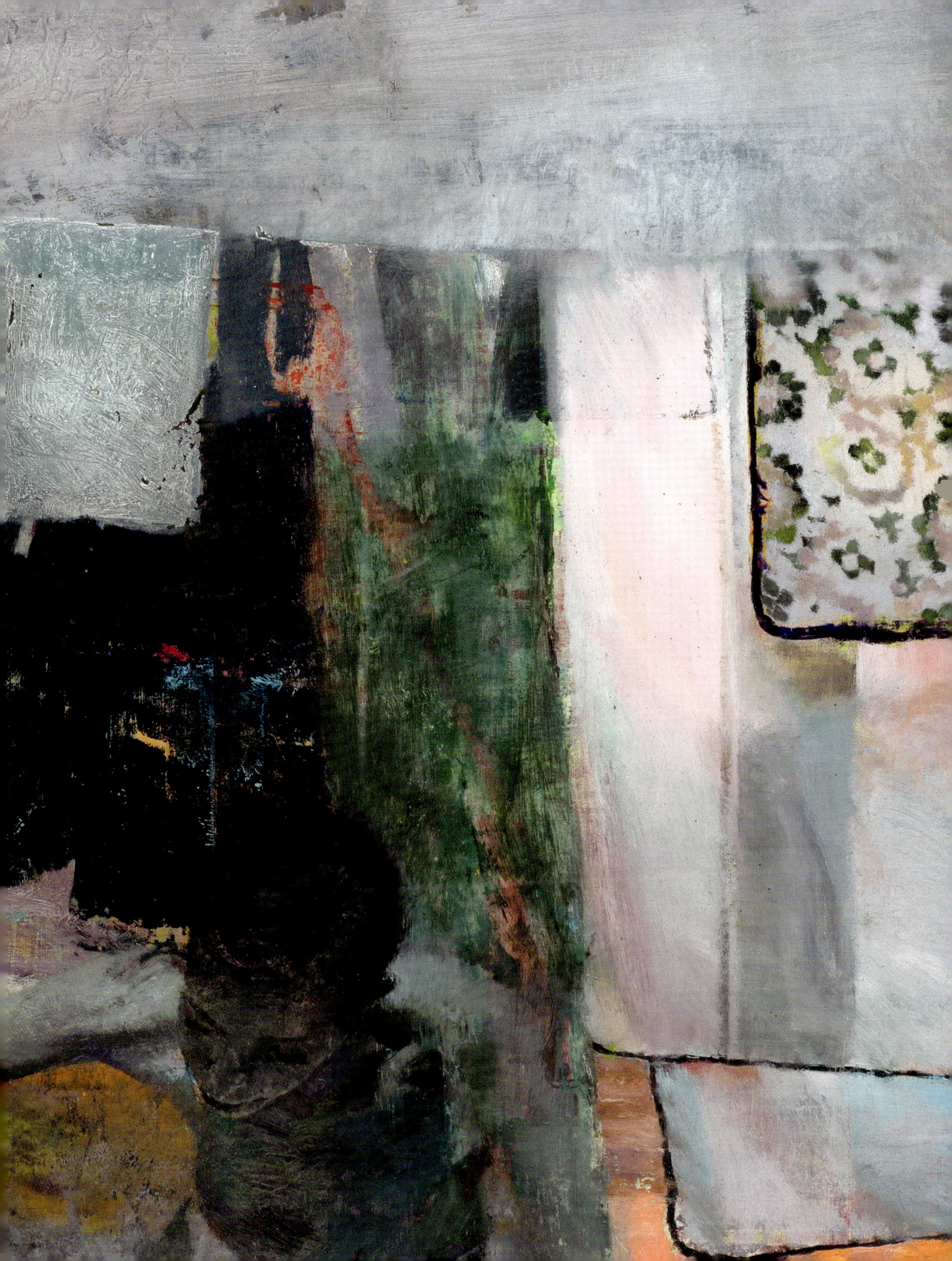

Ryan Mosley

Sunflower King, 2025
Oil on canvas
100 × 80 cm
39⅜ × 31½ in.

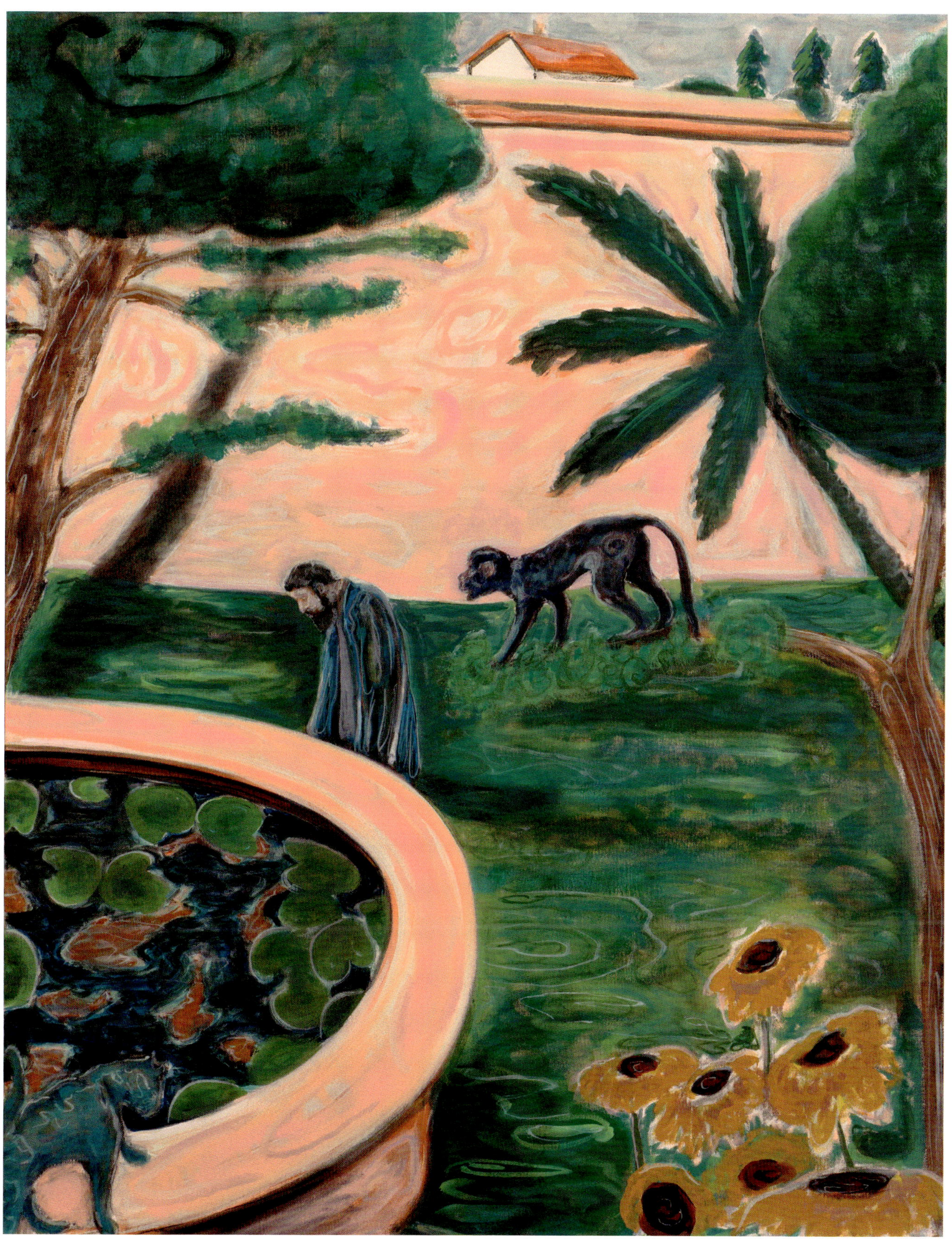

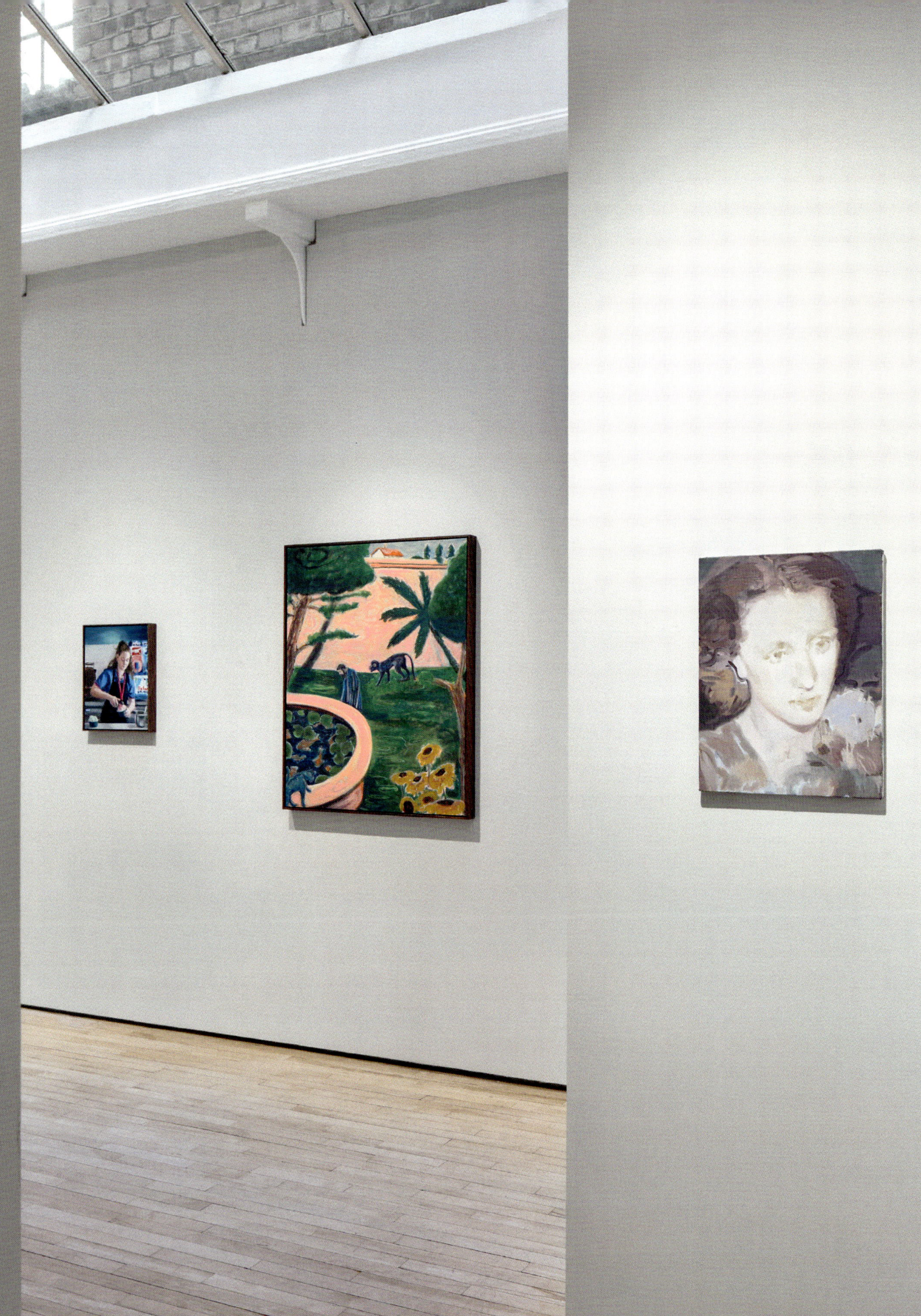

Cara Nahaul

Reverie #12, 2025
Oil on paper
65 × 50 cm
25⅝ × 19¾ in.

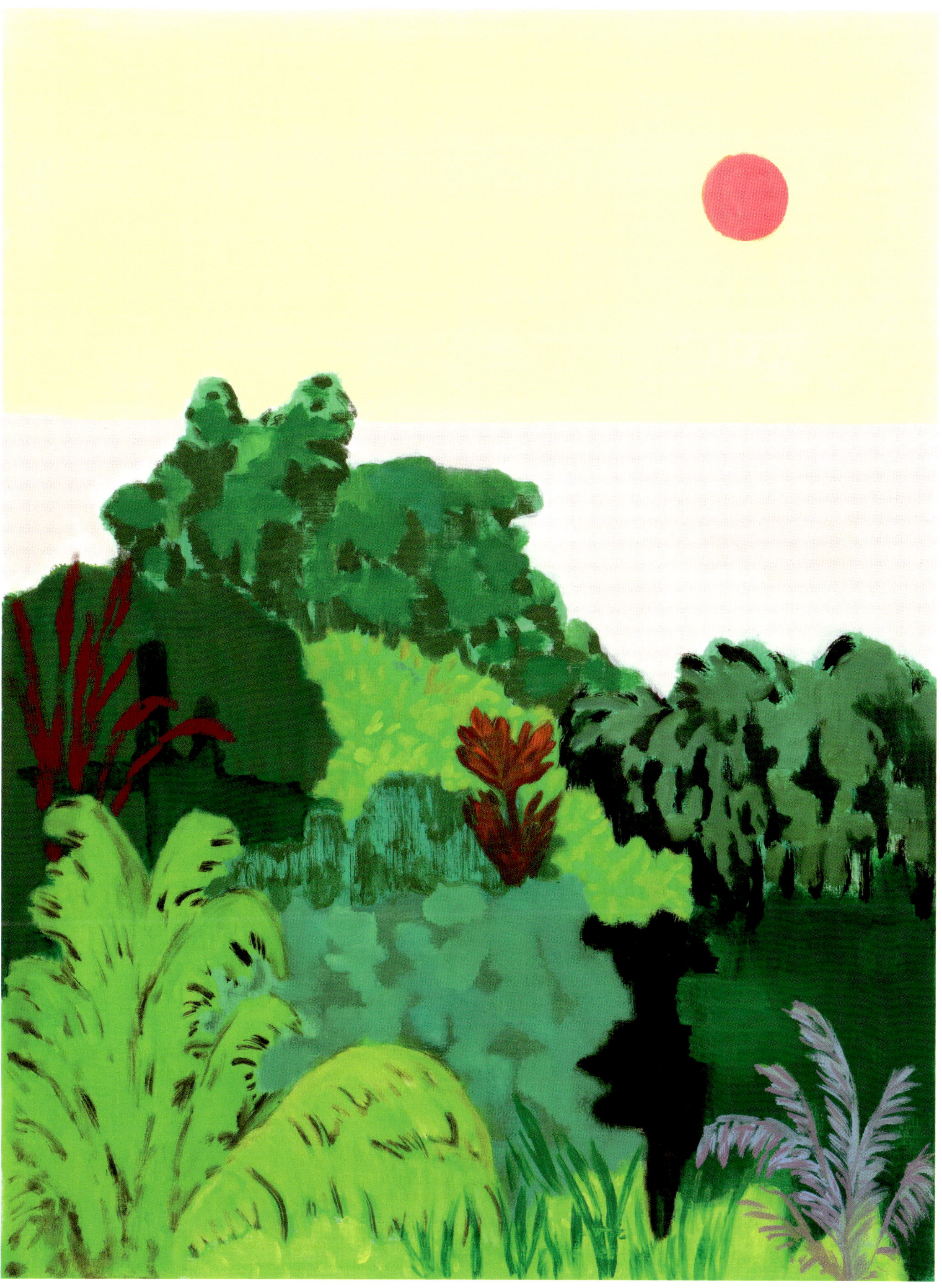

David Price

*Vertumnus and Pomona after
Anthony van Dyck*, 2025
Oil on canvas
40 × 50 cm
15¾ × 19¾ in.

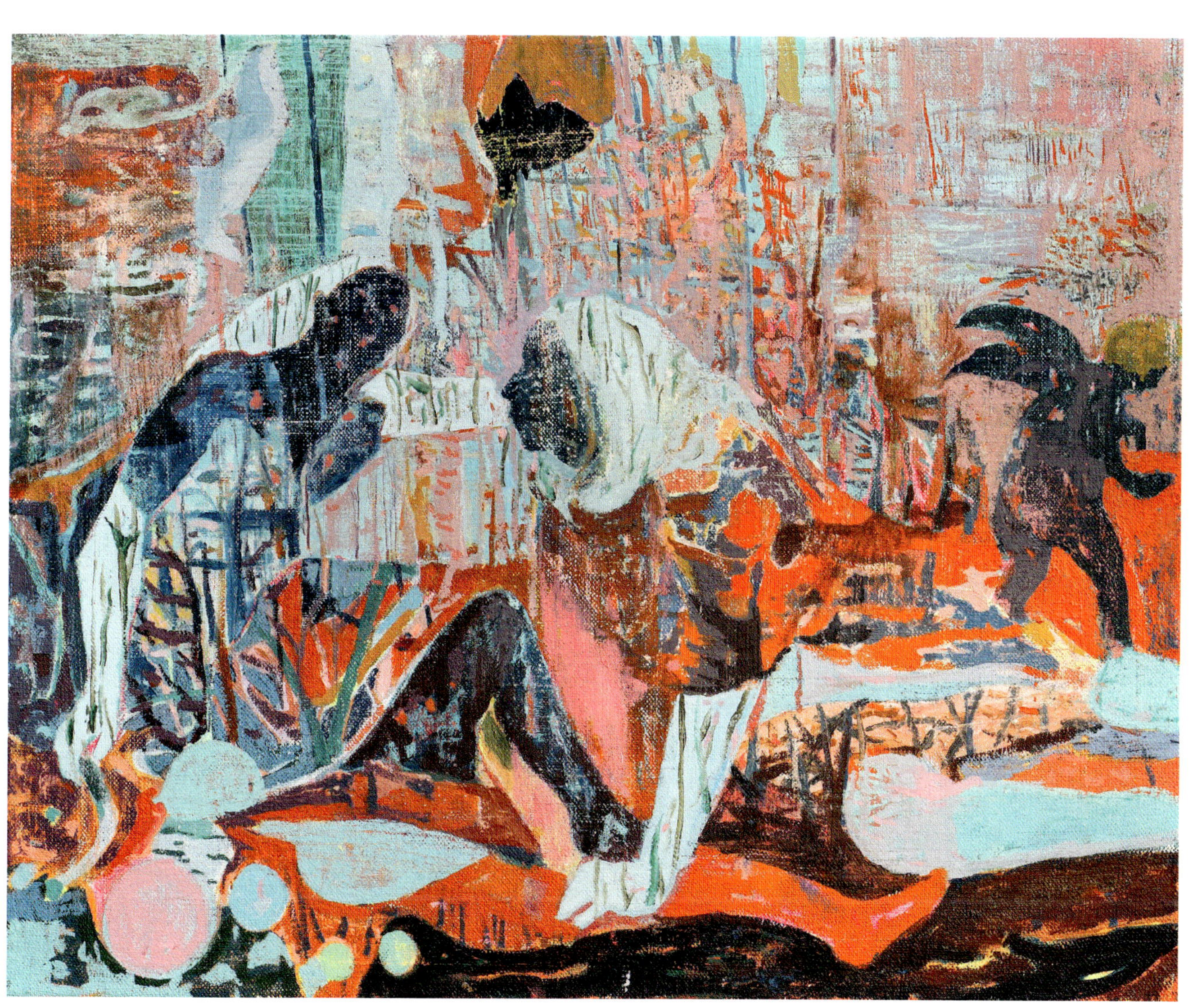

Gideon Rubin

Untitled, 2025
Oil on linen on board
50 × 40 cm
19¾ × 15¾ in.

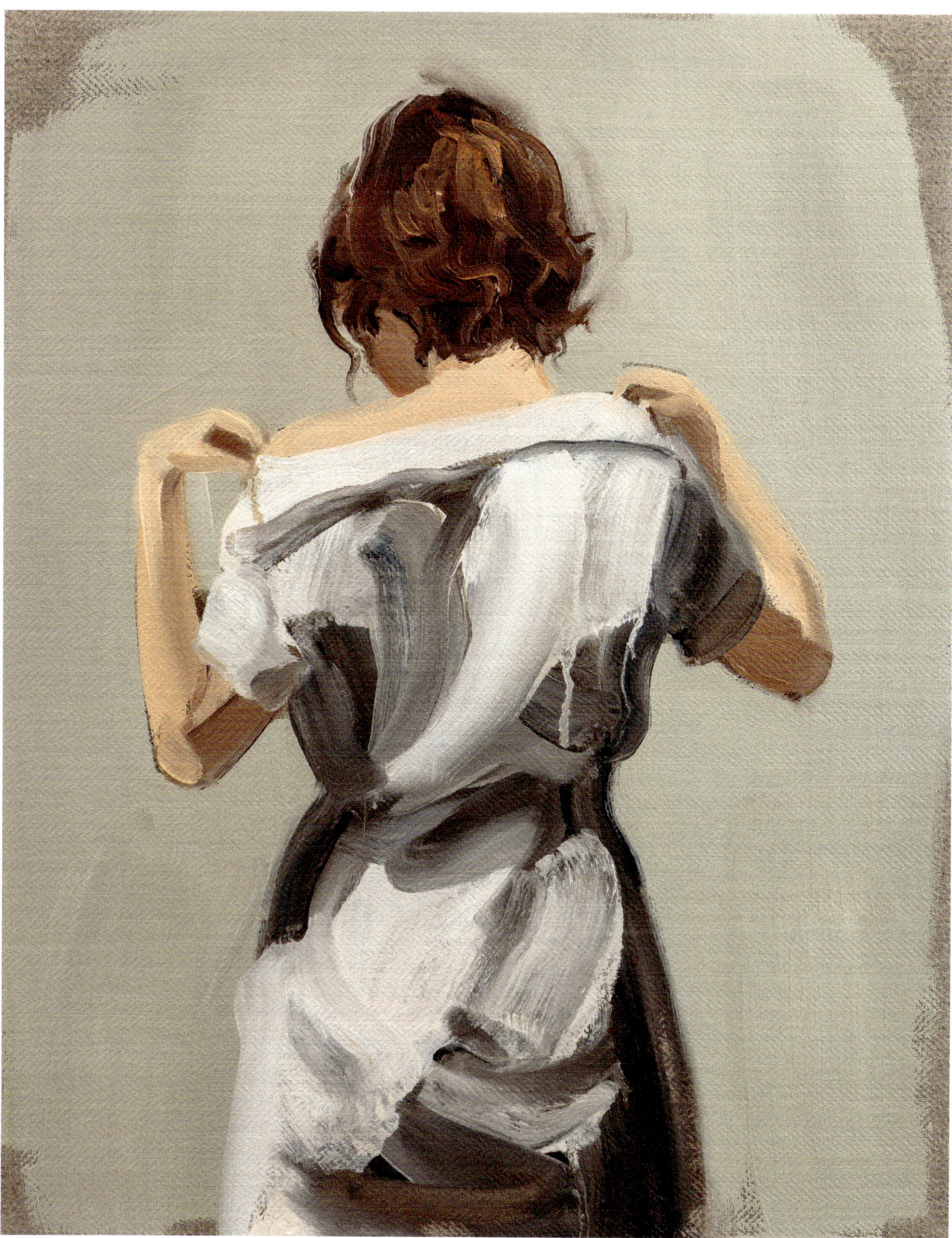

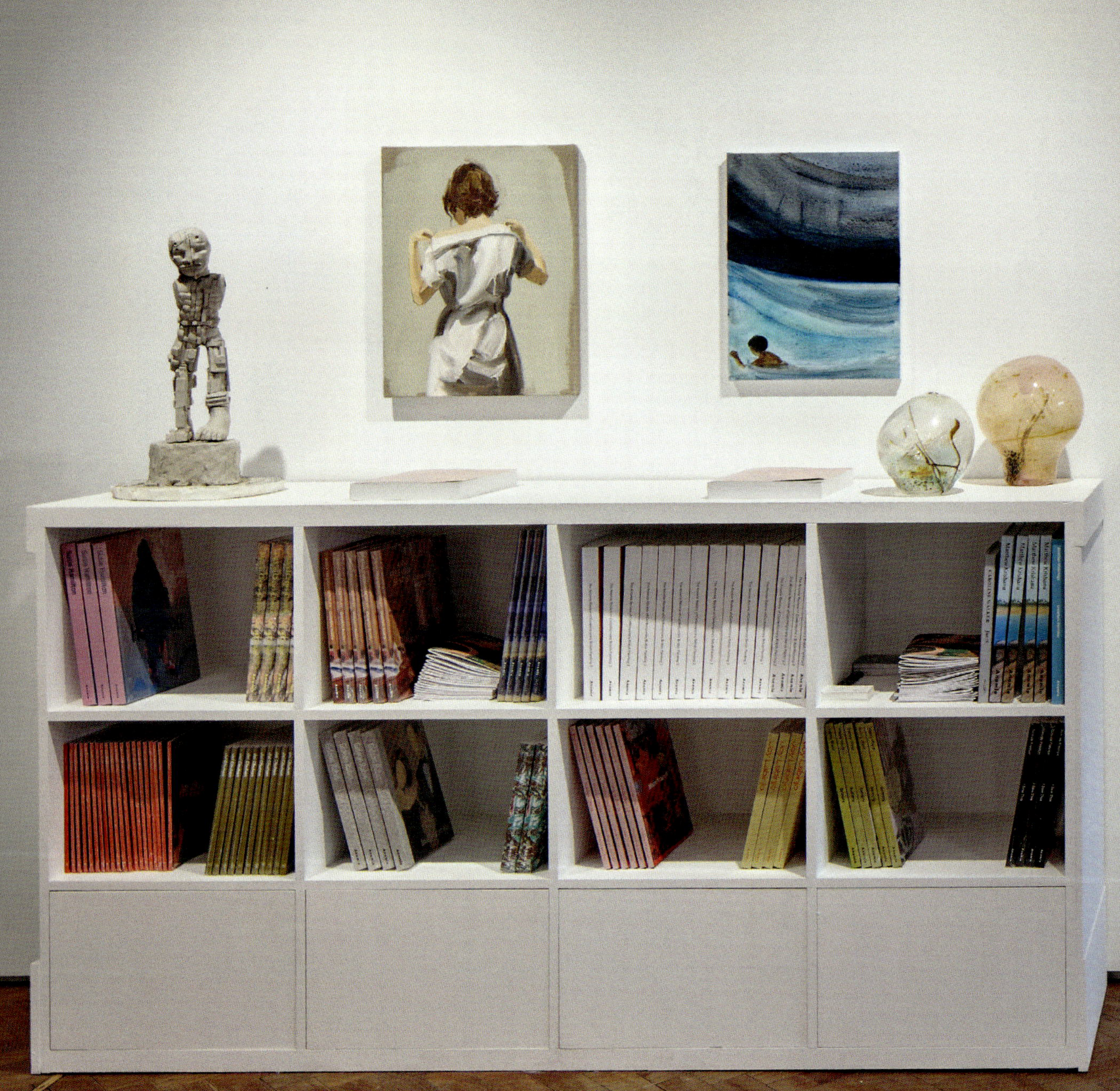

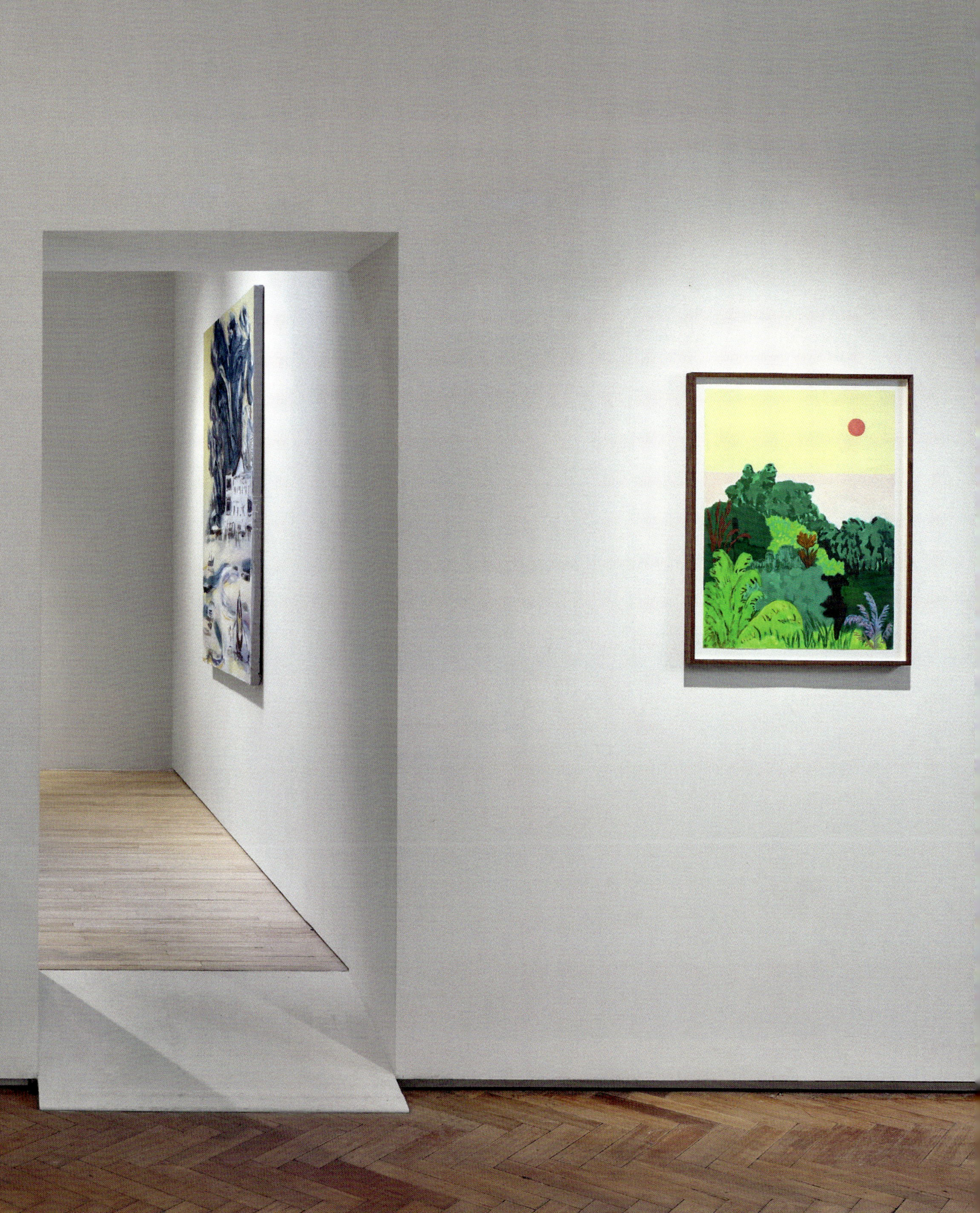

Caroline Walker

Scoops, 2025
Oil on board
43 × 35 cm
16⅞ × 13¾ in.

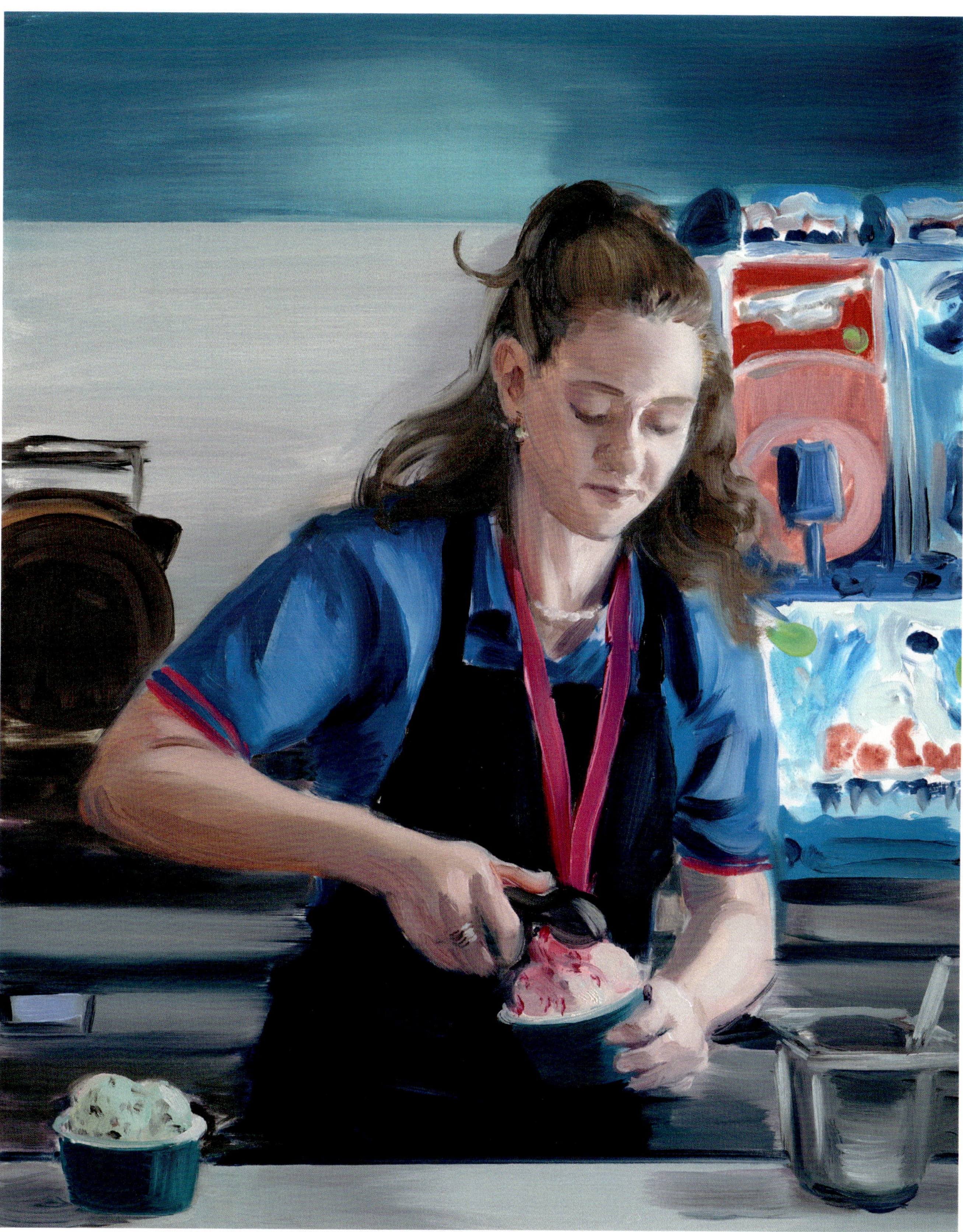

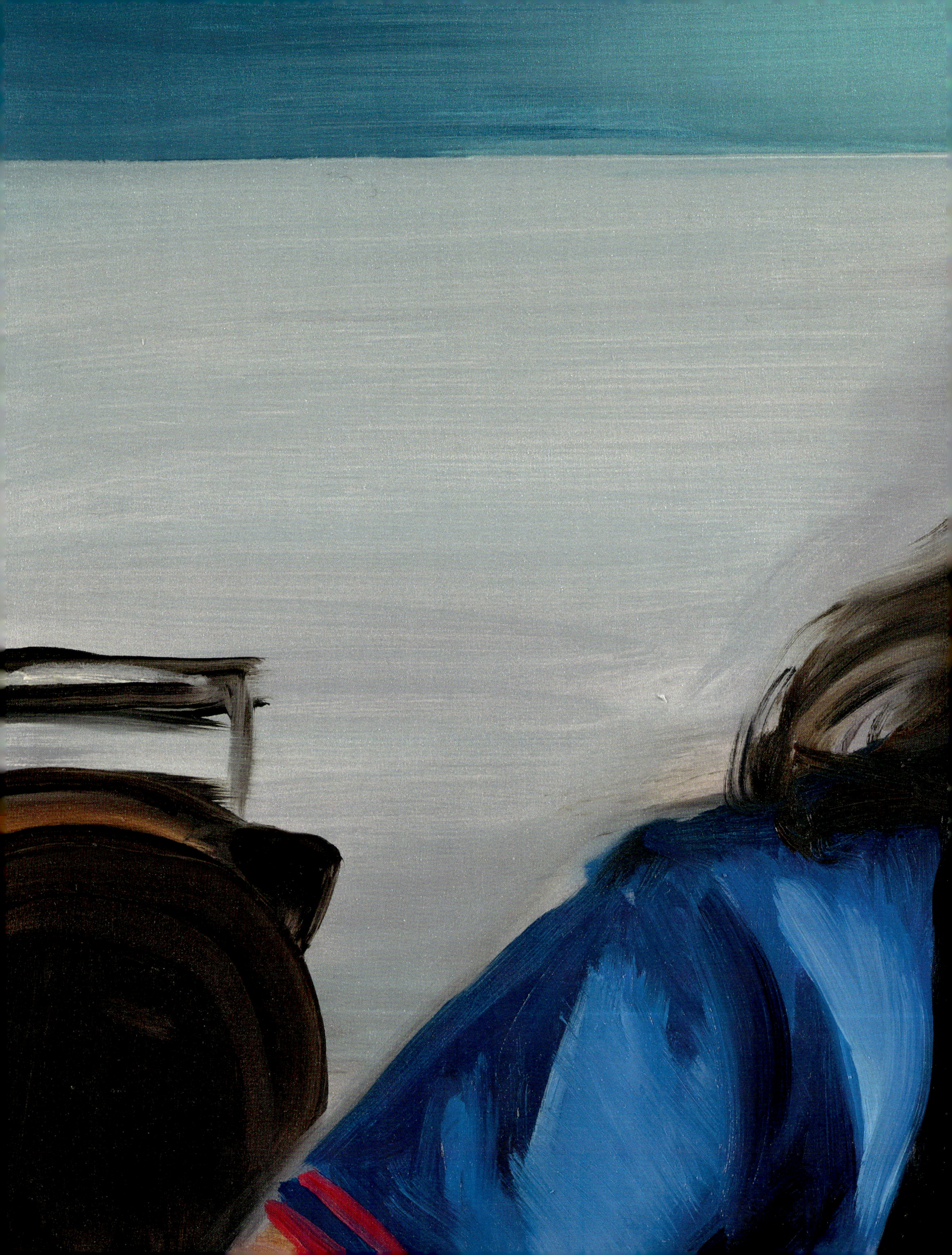

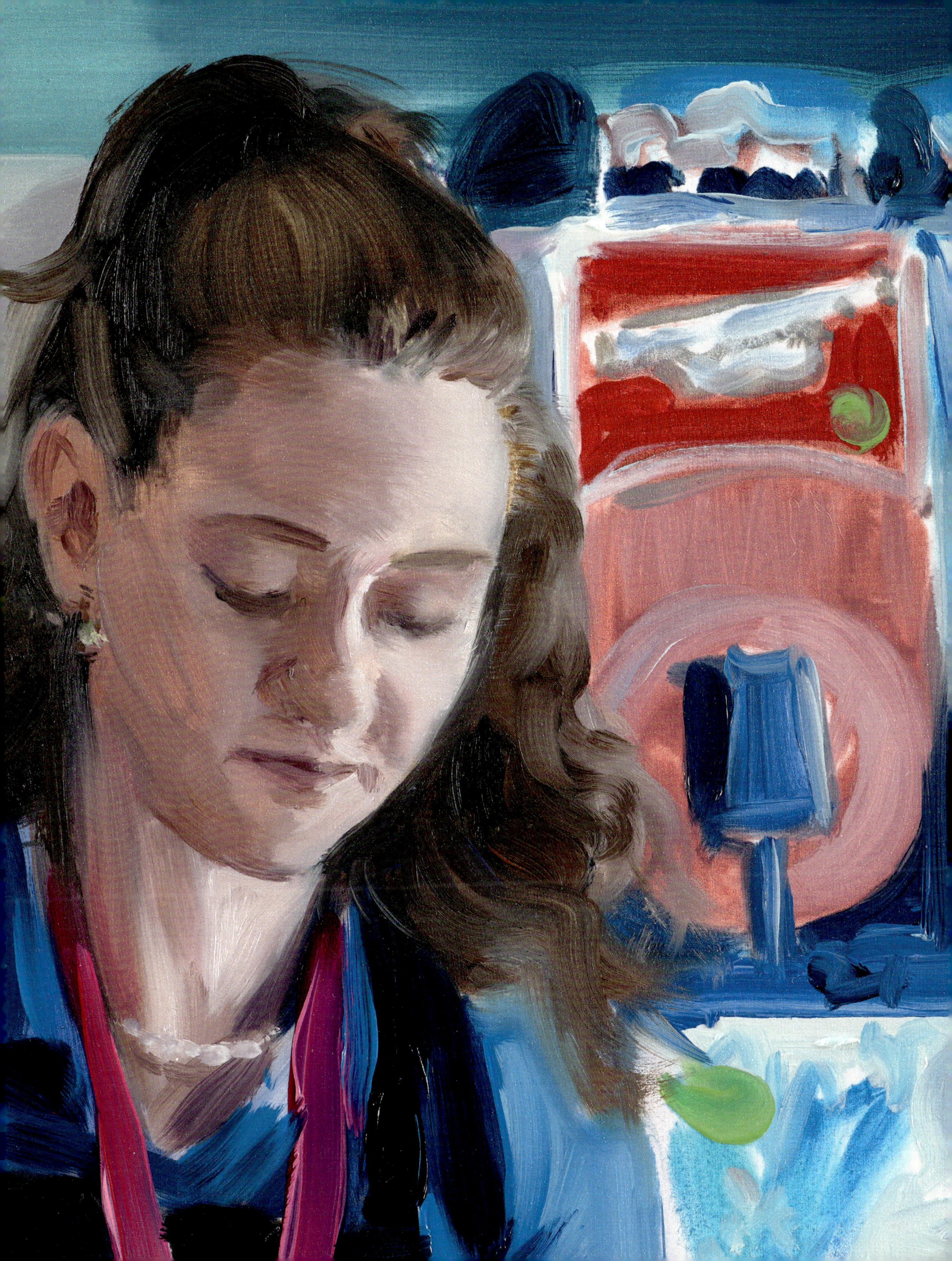

Jonathan Wateridge

Long Weekend, 2025
Oil on linen
169.5 × 120.5 cm
66¾ × 47½ in.

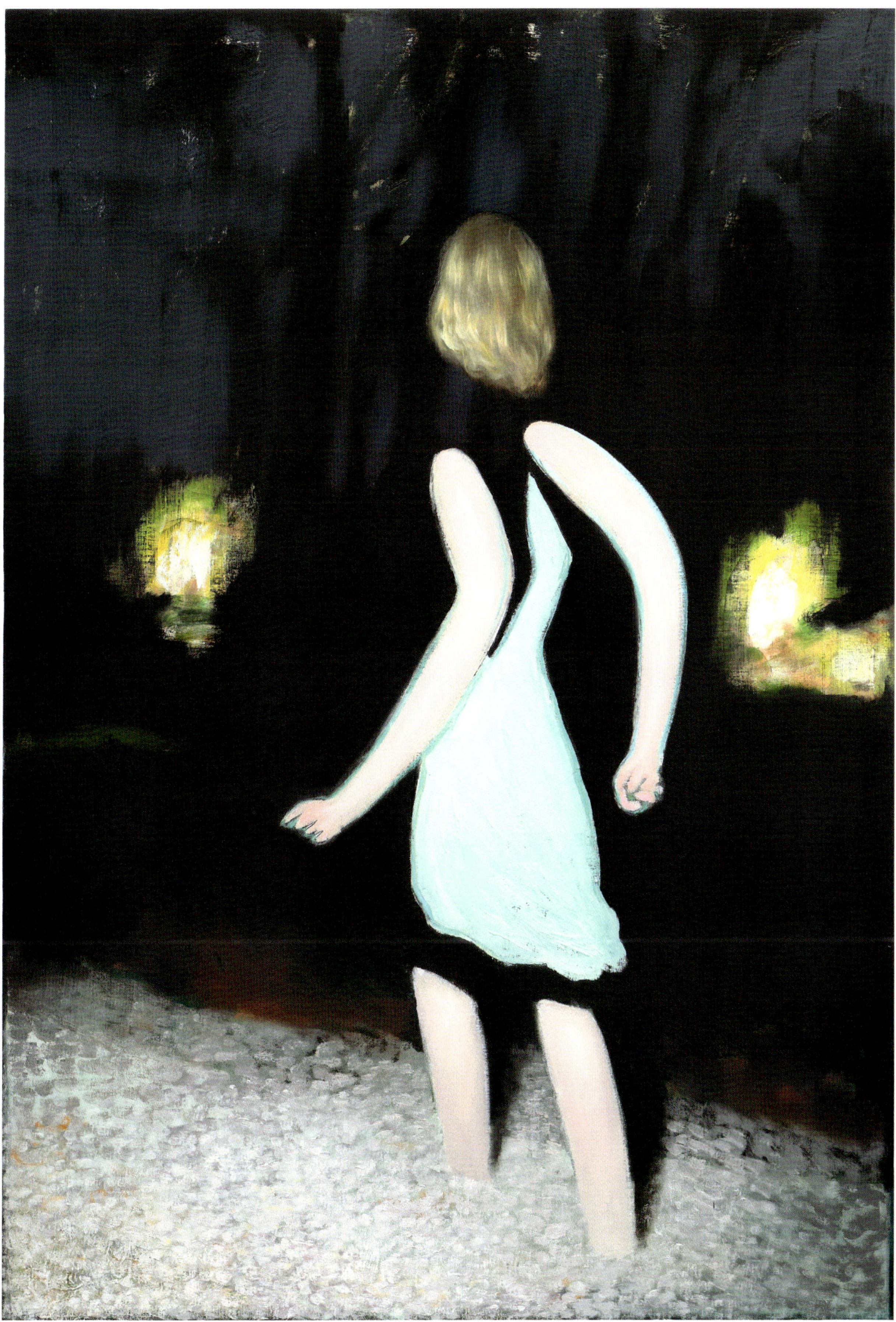

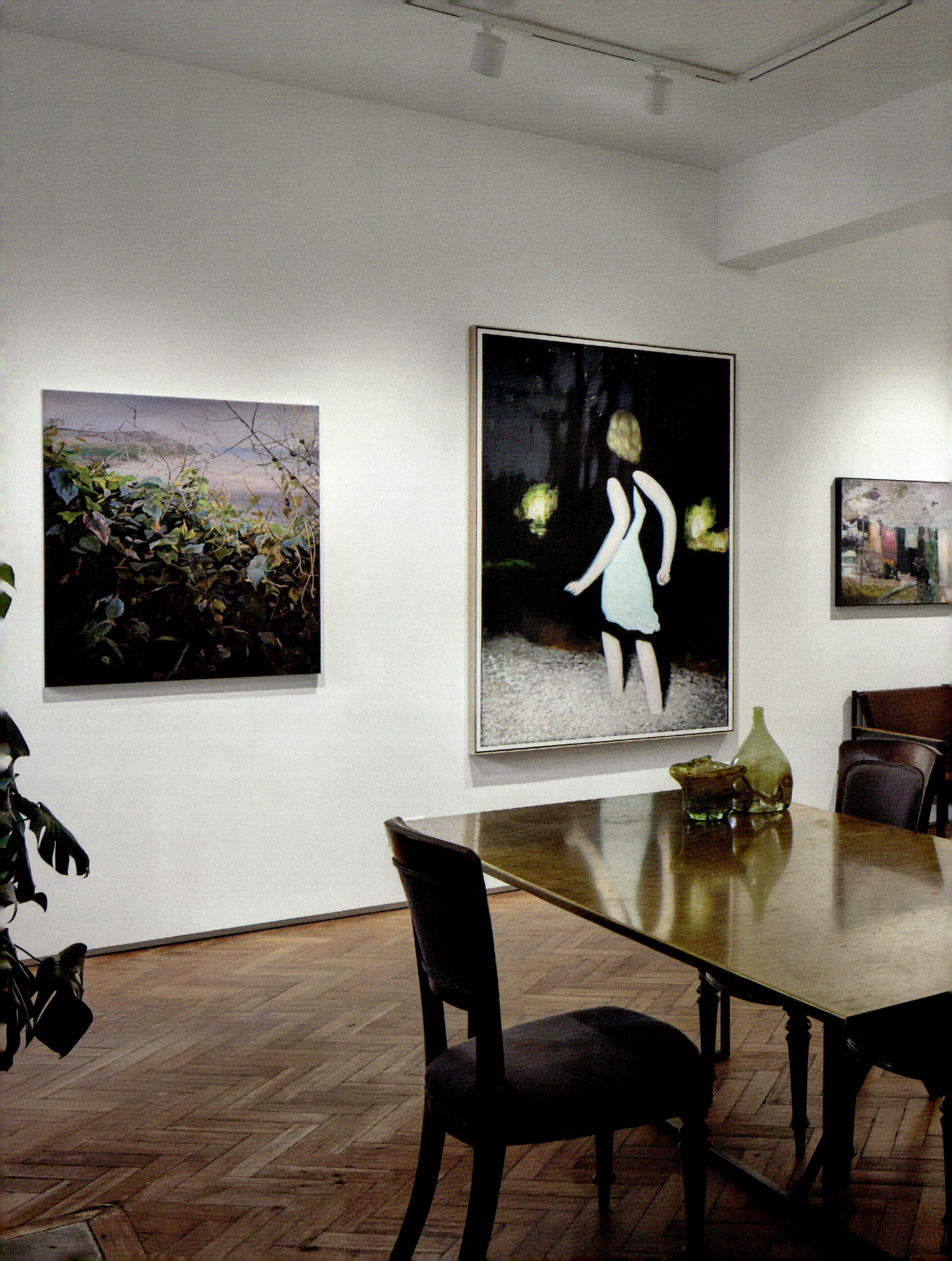

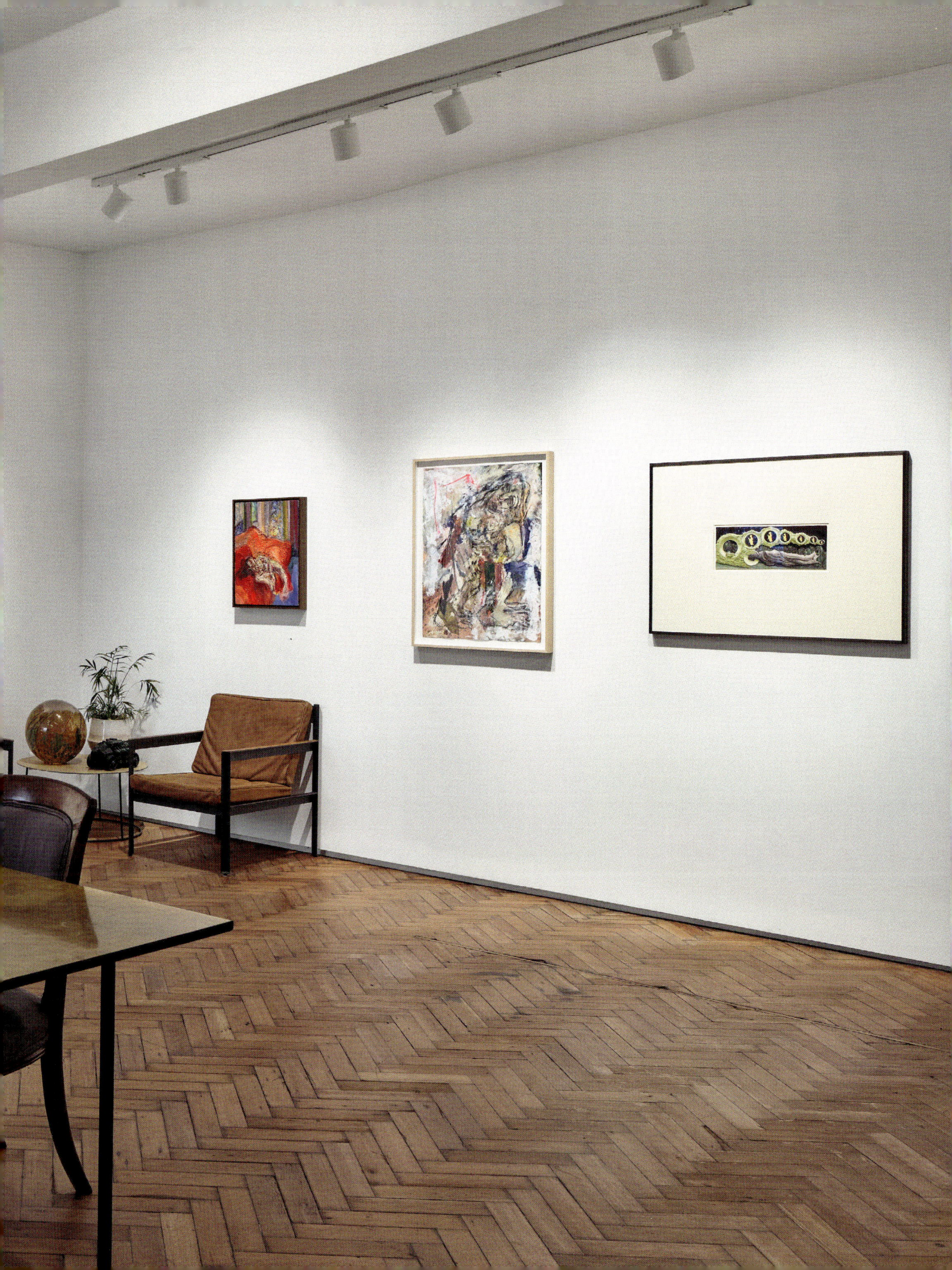

SUMMER

© 2025 Co-published by Frestonian Gallery, London, and Anomie Publishing, London

Texts © their respective authors

Editors
Matt Incledon and Matt Price

Design
Joe Gilmore

Proofreading
William Lambie

Printed by YouLovePrint

With special thanks to:
Tarami Awosile, Leo Babsky, Summer Joseph, Tatiana Lowther-Pinkerton, Coco Price

(Trade edition)

ISBN: 978-1-910221-71-6